Maneuver Management:

Planning and Communication
for Business Success

A Warriors Guide Book
By Mike Ognek

Table of Contents

Introduction

Searching for Success

What is the goal of success in business? I'll tell you that mine is success in my personal life. Certainly, you could argue that both are attainable without the other- they are not mutually dependent. That's true for some people, but not for me. I suspect many of you are the same as I am.

I am driven to create greater and greater success in my businesses in order to create the resources for personal success. Are they the same thing? For some, business success and personal success is the exact same thing. Again- not for me.

Personal success for me is, quite frankly, being a great dad, husband, brother, son, and friend. It's also helping others achieve their own success- whatever that might be. My company, The Warriors Group, allows me to accomplish the latter, but there's more to that. Success is different for everyone and it's not necessarily linked to business. Perhaps it's building a school, feeding the hungry, or coaching their kid's sports team.

Could I be personally successful without business success? Yes, but not to the exact terms of how I define my personal success. Being successful in business allows me to be personally successful by having the flexibility to be at my children's events, provide a good education, and support my wife on those days where the kids are driving her crazy- and believe me they do. It also allows me to set and support my own priorities. That might sound simple, but I know it's not.

What do I mean by that? Ever since my first daughter was born, she was my number one priority. Of course, the others followed and are now also. Even though she was my top priority, I was just out of the Corps and trying to make my way in my own business. Although she remained number one, spending time at home didn't support that priority. I had to make that business a success. I didn't have any savings or a paycheck- everything that came in the door was a direct result of my actions or failure to take action. It was all on the line.

Just like so many other small business owners, I struggled to figure things out. Even though I had extensive experience managing and leading people and projects, I had a tough time cracking the nut on running a civilian business.

I did what so many others do- I read books, scoured the web, sought advice, and grinded away. I still felt like I was getting nowhere fast.

Fourteen months after starting my first post Corps business, my daughter turned one. She was the most adorable, wonderful, funny, and loving person I had ever seen. She was my daughter, she was one year old, but I didn't know anything about her. I was working 7 days a week- gone before she woke up and back after she was asleep. All I had to go on was the occasional night where she wouldn't sleep, lots of pictures (without me), and the sound of her in the background as I had yet another "conversation" with my wife about why I wouldn't be home for dinner.

That day, her birthday, was the biggest turning point in my business life and one of the biggest in my personal life. I questioned a lot of things over the next few days. I wondered why I was doing what I was doing. I wondered if it was worth it. I wanted to provide a wonderful life for my daughter and wife, but it was turning out to be the opposite. I needed to realize that our wonderful life had to have me in it. One of the reasons I left the Corps was to be there for my family. Oddly enough, I wasn't.

The answer I came up with was, "No, it's not worth it." My family was much more important to me than succeeding in business. It was time for a change. That change required some major decisions.

I decided that I was going to support my priorities- I was going to be there for my wife and kids. There were no other options. So, I could hang up the entrepreneurial hat and get a job or unscrew my business and myself. I really considered the earlier, but in the end it just wasn't me. I made the very clear decision that I was going to succeed at both, but never at the expense of my family. Instead of my personal life suffering at the hand of my business, my business success was going to support my personal success.

Immediately after committing to my decision, I did an inventory of what I had in my success toolbox. I looked for the things that had made me successful at things I had done in the past and how I could apply them to my business. What I realized was that I had benched the most valuable player on my team- my military experience. I had a wealth of real world experience and I wasn't employing it.

What was so different about civilian business and the military? Well, there were a few things- namely no one was shooting at anyone. So, okay, there are a lot of differences, but there are also a lot of similarities. At the most basic level, there was a mission. That mission had objectives and I had limited resources to apply to accomplish that mission.

Most significantly, I had only so much time and money and when that ran out, my mission was at risk. I had to lead my people to make my vision a reality and simultaneously manage my resources and systems.

More than a light bulb went off- it was a damn Vegas light show. I had everything I needed to succeed in business- no matter what that business was. I just had to adapt it for business use. That's exactly what I did.

I refined it as I went and put it to use in business after business with the same results- success. Success, in business, that allowed me to have the personal success that I really wanted most of all. I know it works and I know it will work for you too- if you apply it.

If you don't have clear list of priorities, it's time you make one. From that, you can make some decisions about what is really important in your life and how you are going to support those priorities. It might be time to take an inventory as well- what do you have in your success toolbox?

We have an article posted in the Warriors Library (Click Resources at www.thewarriorsgroup.com) about "Legacy." In it, I talk about the 4 greatest gifts one person can give to another. I recommend reading it as you take a look at your own priorities- I hope it adds some clarity and food for thought in that process for you.

Once I figured this out and found success, I began to launch other enterprises. As I did that, I studied others and talked with a number of fellow entrepreneurs. I was struck by the lack of consistency and structure that many of these small and medium sized businesses suffered from; it went beyond just having the knowledge- it was a matter of planning, communication, and execution.

They tended to manage almost by hopeful osmosis, where management principles and processes are diffused across the organization informally and in many cases, haphazardly. It is also typically true that small to mid sized companies lack a formal process to plan and manage effectively. This in turn often leads to inconsistent operational performance, and enterprise-wide systemic problems that tend to worsen over time.

Now that I understood the correlation between my service as a Marine Officer and the business world, this lack of structure was very clear to me. Very often, there weren't even any plans in place and if there were, no one understood them.

As I thought about it more, everything I was doing could be institutionalized. With slight adaptations, even those without any military experience or exposure to the tools and concepts could learn them and employ them to great effect. This is not only true for the methodologies, but also for the application of the warfighting doctrine- the mindset, strategy, and tactics that helped make my businesses successful.

From this, Maneuver Management was born. In all honesty, it was an ugly baby at first as I took what I knew and made it into a system for others, even those without previous exposure to the military. As I learned lessons, I adapted the system and in the process refined even my own business operations. The information contained in this book is the result of years of refinement, execution, analysis, and further refinement. In fact, the information contained herein has been completely re-written, re-organized, and edited with feedback from readers like you in order to make it easier to understand and implement. What you are about to read is a proven methodology for success.

The idea of using military doctrine for business is nothing new. The Japanese are a prime example of this- they dominate several industries and they got there using a strategy based on warfighting. Many of you have been exposed to the business value of Sun Tzu's Art of War. The idea works, there's evidence of that. So, why don't more organizations, large and small, use that type of operating doctrine? It's because they don't know how to implement and maintain it; they don't know where to start.

If one person in an organization is working in that manner, even if it's the CEO, it won't make an enormous difference. If, however, the entire organization operates from a framework of success based on the tools, planning process, and mindset of a successful military organization and then communicates that effectively- success becomes a replicable process instead of a fluke.

This isn't to say that your organization needs to become a para-military force. Not at all. What I am saying is that your organization needs to adapt the same will to win that is found in the military. This is achieved through the proper culture, but culture doesn't just happen. The military culture is based on a history that your organization cannot replicate. Your organization has its own history though and that is a part of your culture. Military culture is also based on a methodology for operating. That is something you can replicate. The way to begin that is to begin planning and communicating with clarity using the tools in this book. The simple fact that you and your employees will have a greater understanding of their mission, roles, and responsibilities will create great focus and shift your culture immediately.

That's not the end though. You will need to continue to develop your culture by decentralizing decision-making, promoting and rewarding success driven behaviors, and growing through lessons learned. In fact, the continued shift in culture and the survival of the tools in your organization are mutually dependent. If you implement the tools in this book, you will see an immediate shift in performance and culture that lead to greater success. If you fail to develop that shift, the tools will not help you any further.

Does all of this sound like it's too much? Too Difficult? Well, I'm here to tell you it isn't. It's completely within your reach- better planning, communication, execution, and strategy. There is a catch though. There's always a catch, isn't there? The catch here is that you have to want to help yourself and your organization, no matter how small or large it may be.

That's it. That's the catch. It may sound easy enough, but I can tell you from years of experience in dealing with people and businesses, once the belief in being able to succeed is gone, no one can restore that but the person who has lost it.

I know, "great motivational attitude, Mike." Lucky for both of us, I'm not a "make you feel better about yourself" kind of guy. I'm a "help you succeed" kind of guy. You won't find any pep talks about how good you are at what you do or what value you bring to the world; that motivation comes from within.

What you will find in the following pages is a proven methodology for succeeding in your business.

As you implement these tools and methodologies, my Warriors Group team and I are here to help. If you have a question or need help implementing Maneuver Management, contact us via The Warriors Group website. Although I personally receive piles of email everyday, I do attempt to respond to as many questions as I can.

Chapter 1

Maneuver Management

Why is it that so many businesses fail? Is it because the owners and managers lack the skills necessary to effectively operate them? Is it that the products and services being offered are not in high enough demand, are not being conveyed properly, or that the concept itself is flawed? The truth is that it's a combination of all those things and more. So, what's the answer? How do we create success?

That's a doozy of a question. I would love to tell you that this book will help you find success no matter what. Regrettably, that's not the case. The good news is that there is a good reason for that and knowing it will help you succeed.

The tools, processes, and concepts presented here work. It's that simple. What this system, or any system for that matter, can't do is remove the human element from your business. The human element is what will determine whether or not your business is a success.

So, you might ask, why do I need this book then, if the human element is what will determine success? Great question. The answer is that this system, inclusive of the processes, tools, and concepts, will help you control the human element to a greater degree. It is meant to create the clearest picture of the operating environment possible for you, your employees, and your overall business. By doing that, coupled with clear and controlled execution, we can mitigate many of the risks associated with a free-willed human element.

As I said though, we can't eliminate the effects of it. You and your employees will have to make decisions and choose courses of action based on the information you have at the time. Those decisions will be based on myriad factors, including education, training, experience, will, and even mood. The latter two of which are variables that cannot be quantified, as they are completely subjective. I cannot, necessarily, fully understand the emotions you experience as they occur within you and within you alone. I may be able to relate through similar experience, but I will never be able to fully understand the impact of events and influences on you internally.

So, to answer the question at hand, how do we create success- we create success by understanding the environment in which we operate as best we can and applying systematic, controlled activities to influence that environment while creating and exploiting opportunity within it.

Remember, the operating environment is internal as much as it is external. Your employees and other resources contribute to your internal environment equally as much as the market and competitors create pressures (positive and negative) on your operations.

It's important to note that I said, "as best we can," when referring to understanding our environment. In a perfect world, we would have all of the information we need to make a correct decision. Well, the world is far from perfect and we'll never have all of the information we want to make decisions.

What is Maneuver Management?

Maneuver Management is a system- a compilation of tools, processes, techniques, and concepts you can use to achieve success in your business. It is based on the methodologies learned by Marines, both Officers and Senior Enlisted. There are many similarities between business and the military that allow the translation of operating concepts relatively seamlessly. There are also many differences and, where applicable, those differences have been rectified by adapting the core operating model of the Marine Corps to fit civilian business.

Also contained in Maneuver Management are concepts and tools developed outside of the military framework. Although they would work equally as well in the military, they are not drawn directly from military operating techniques. It would be naïve to state these elements are free from any military training influence. That mindset is part of me and is, therefor, inseparable from my business-operating model.

Beyond the operating components I will present to you, there is an additional aspect of Maneuver Management that is indispensible to employing it to success. That is the concept of Maneuver.

The Marine Corps operates from a doctrine called Maneuver Warfare. We will discuss this in greater detail throughout the book, but it's important to understand the relevancy here before going forward.

Maneuver is more than just moving your "forces." It is as much, if not more, about how you allocate and apply your resources as it is about how you move them. It is about identifying opportunity and exploiting it equally as much as it is about identifying areas of resistance and avoiding them.

Maneuver Warfare, and therefor Maneuver Management, is based on several key concepts. Certainly, almost all of them apply to civilian business without adaptation, save changing some terminology to reflect non-combat operations. It's from these concepts that the actual tools and processes are born.

Understand that it is not my intent to suggest business should be conducted with the same intensity and consequence as war. That would be absurd. What I do aim to do is provide you with tools and processes that have been adapted from military operating methodologies and are proven to be successful. I aim to help you succeed, as I have, using the system of Maneuver Management.

The Levels of Maneuver Management

In an understanding that not all businesses require all of the processes contained in the Maneuver Management System or are necessarily prepared to enter into such a robust planning cycle, I have broken the system into three levels. Each level is more in depth and adds components to the process. As new concepts and tools are introduced, they will feel familiar to you because they are a progression of earlier components.

In addition to the actual tools and components, in higher levels I introduce basic operating concepts and principles that will help you refine you business strategy. Coupled together with the tools I provide, they complete the Maneuver Management System.

In Level I, I introduce the concept of Battlespace. This is a pre-requisite for operating your business from a more strategic perspective and will set the stage for more productive planning and execution. Because decisions inherently involve risk, especially in business, I talk about the difference between taking risks and making gambles. At the culmination of Level I, I show you the most powerful tool in the Maneuver Management System: The 5 Paragraph Plan, which we abbreviate as the 5P. You will use the 5P to plan and communicate effectively, which will allow you and your organization to operate from a common picture, with common goals and understanding.

The 5P is an adaptation of the Marine Corp's 5 Paragraph Order, the tool for issuing orders to units and personnel for execution and/or breakdown for further planning. The Marine Corps uses a very intensive planning process, aptly called the Marine Corps Planning Process, or MCPP, to arrive at the substance to populate the 5 Paragraph Order. Yes, I am aware of the fact that the acronym sounds like a fast food item you do not want to order, but it is one of the most effective planning processes in the world. Most businesses will not engage in such a rigorous planning process to arrive at a plan and that's okay.

The 5 Paragraph Order is a template meant to be filled in with the necessary information and direction for the larger plan's execution. Therefore, it is one of the most refined methods for communicating plans and directions available. As a necessary part of completing a 5 Paragraph Order, the author is forced to consider elements of their plan that are otherwise easily overlooked, even after engaging in a comprehensive planning session. It's for that reason that the 5 Paragraph format is so valuable, in and of itself, as a planning tool.

Our adaptation of the 5 Paragraph Order, the 5 Paragraph Plan (the 5P) utilizes the overall format of the original Marine Corps version, but refines it even further for businesses. We maintain the integrity of the format which, again, is one of the most refined communication methods available, while adapting it for use as both a planning tool and a vehicle for effectively communicating your plan and decisions.

Level II introduces three key operating concepts: The Leadership Success Model, The Management/Leadership Quadrant, and the Business Cycle Pendulum. These three concepts will help you succeed by acting on purpose, allocating human resource's appropriately, and understanding how to plan for changes in your business operations, respectively.

Level III introduces the operating principles of Maneuver Management and the full Warriors Guide Planning Process (WGPP). It's here that you will learn the robust planning and execution process that will enable you and your organization to implement a full cycle planning system for all levels of operations and contingencies.

The WGPP is for organizations requiring a more robust planning cycle and methodology. For smaller organizations or dealing with alligators at the bow, I not only expect you to, but also recommend you skip that section for the time being. Come back to it if you have a need or when you desire to engage in more robust and complicated process.

We'll close with a brief chapter on essential leadership characteristics that I hope will help you refine your leadership and focus on three key attributes that will help you succeed at whatever you do. Let's begin.

LEVEL I

Chapter 2

Know Your Battlespace

A Battlespace is where we operate. It's not just the geography of where we operate however. It includes the resources, opponents, stakeholders, as well as the economic, political, meteorological, and even temporal aspects of the arena in which we operate. It's a literal reference to a specific space and time as well as a representation of the tangible and intangible influences that shape the environment. It is, in entirety, our operating environment.

In order to visualize and understand your Battlespace, I suggest you create a Battlespace map. A Battlespace map is simply a visual representation of your operating environment, including all relevant aspects of your business.

Battlespace mapping works without regard to the size of your business. If you are a sole proprietor and only employee, it works just as effectively as if you run a multi-national corporation with 50k employees. I know that because I personally use it in businesses of different sizes, have been part of its use in multi-national military operations, and have even been a party in its use for the planning and execution of the Marine Corps Marathon. I've succeeded with it personally and been a part of successful organizations that use it.

There is no difference in concept here between the Marine Corps and civilian business. Your geography contains your physical market. Your resources are your people, supplies, equipment, and products. Your opponents are your competition. Your stakeholders are your customers, shareholders, and employees. External economic and political conditions will critically affect your strategy and implementation as well as your available resources.

Meteorology represents the physical environment—will the weather hinder your logistics or operations? Does the weather represent an internal surface or gap (a surface is a strength, a gap is a weakness-more on this later)? Is inclement weather an opportunity relative to your product or service or is it a critical vulnerability?

Time, the temporal aspect of a Battlespace, affects everything. What is your time horizon compared to your competition? How long is your decision making cycle? How does time affect the relevancy and effectiveness of your marketing and product?

All of these things build a clearer picture of our Battlespace. The more clearly defined our Battlespace is, the more clearly we see it and, therefore, the more effectively we can operate within it and influence it.

For example, a fast food operator contemplating the development of an expansion plan that includes the opening of new stores throughout a defined region would be very concerned with the geography of the Battlespace in which he plans to operate. In this case, the physical lay of the land—highways, population centers, shopping areas and so forth— would all be particularly relevant. Additionally, demographic and psychographic data would form part of the Battlespace, along with competitors and their respective offerings.

A consumer products company trying to build market share might also be concerned about geography, but at a higher level. Sales figures by region would be important, as would distribution channels within those regions. In this case, however, the physical lay of the land would be far less important. As with the fast food operator, all of the factors that define the company's target market would be part of the Battlespace.

Yet another example would be a manufacturer considering changes to an assembly line. In this business case, the assembly line itself, and every aspect of it, as well as all of the channels that feed material and maintain the machinery would form the perimeter of the Battlespace for planning purposes.

It is important to be cognizant of the fact that you are always engaged in the Battlespace, in every aspect of your business. This includes everything from administrative function to production, marketing to delivery and customer service. A clear understanding of all your Battlespace is vital to operating effectively and employing resources to maximum effect.

Today most organizations, including the Marine Corps, are faced with including cyberspace in their Battlespace. For the military, this is a literal Battlespace. For businesses, it's most often a component of their Battlespace in the form of marketing, sales, and communication.

A Competitive Edge

In civilian business, Battlespace mapping is an exceptionally useful tool for strategic analysis and planning. Using a Battlespace map to visually depict the Battlespace—even if geography is irrelevant—allows the planner to develop a visual-spatial relationship between planning elements, and to be able to grasp and understand data and relationships much more quickly than simply by reading it.

This tool is amazingly simple and incredibly useful—but businesses rarely use it. Mostly because they don't know they should, but those that do don't understand the value. Even though it's situational awareness 101 for a military mind, mapping the Battlespace first requires an understanding of what a Battlespace is and the linkage between Battlespace and marketplace has to be created.

The concept of developing a Battlespace is one of my favorites because it's a tool that anyone can use right now with immediate results. Properly created, a Battlespace map will add instant clarity to your environment. It's also probably because it reminds me of playing the board game "Risk," which is a great way to describe what you want to create. Think about that game, if you've ever played it. You are able to look at the board and see your forces, your opponent's forces, the geography and "attack" routes as well as the "bonus" in troops you get for full occupation. Keep that in mind and now shift from little plastic men to the operational aspects of your business.

Let's look at a very basic example of using a Battlespace map to start to gain a more thorough understanding. This is a real world use, from one of my own businesses.

This business involves acquiring distressed real estate, otherwise known as foreclosures. That business operates in a large geographic area and has a certain level of resources. Those resources include money, time, people (staff, lawyers, contractors, real estate agents, inspectors, and so on), and materials. We have an effective business model that is extremely profitable and one of the most important factors of our success is our ability to identify opportunities and manage our resources effectively- this is also true for you and any other business.

In the current market, there are an abundance of distressed properties. It is, as we say, a target-rich environment. But overextending could easily bury an organization—engaging in acquisition after acquisition with limited available resources spread across an excessively wide area is inefficient and costly. Projects might be profitable at some level, but they could also be chosen and managed far more efficiently and thus be much more profitable.

Since there are an abundance of assets available for acquisition, it makes sense to map out the prospects in order to get a sense of where they are geographically. Doing this, in turn, exposes areas with high concentrations and low concentrations of prospective properties. This is done on an actual geographic map.

Now, we can overlay our resources and discover a solution that enables us to choose the prospective acquisitions to best apply them to in the most efficient manner. What we are doing is creating a picture of how our Battlespace looks and in doing so we are exposing opportunity and efficiency. Knowing those allows us to better control the Battlespace and economize our forces and efforts.

Next, we overlay market conditions on our Battlespace map and find areas with both a high concentration of prospective properties and favorable market conditions where our resources can more efficiently be employed. From this, we see high turnover markets with greater acquisition prospects where our resources can be efficiently deployed and applied.

Although this may be a very simple example of using the Battlespace concept, its also illustrates its scalability. It works in every situation, in every industry and it can work for you right now. Stop for a minute and think about your Battlespace. The best case is for you to put the book down and go create your own Battlespace map. If you choose to read on and do it at another point, that's fine, just make sure you do this before you do anything else.

This is important because even from a planning perspective, mapping the Battlespace allows the planner to align surfaces and gaps, reinforce advantages and identify weaknesses. It helps the planner to achieve both strategic and tactical situational awareness. It assists with decision-making and extends your time horizon. All of these, allow you to identify and exploit opportunity. I will add it can even be fun.

Mapping Your Battlespace

Friendly

As with the example used above, if your Battlespace includes a physical geography, then start with an actual map. If you can't find a map that displays the area you need, there are websites that allow you to create a custom map and have it printed. This has a few advantages over a stock, store bought map. First, you can reduce clutter by only including information that is relevant to you. If you don't need the name of every little town, don't include it on the map. Conversely, you can typically add data not found on a stock map; information such as income, population, age breakdown, etc. Having this data already printed on your map can help reduce workload and confusion later in your planning and operations.

From there, begin to add representations of data elements that are important factors in your operations. If you are a manufacturer, include factories, ports, warehouses, and processing facilities. If you are a florist, add your shop, distributors, pick up points, daily clients, shipping services, etc. Remember the "Risk" board game.

No matter what the business, if your company owns it, uses it, or relies on it- add it. I suggest that if your organization is larger and/or more complex, utilize overlays. These are sheets that can be, well, over-laid, on your main map. Perhaps one for factories, one for ports, shippers, warehouses, and so on would be appropriate. It all depends on the size and scope of your organizations Battlespace. The more inclusive or expansive it is, the more elements you'll need to create a comprehensive picture. Alternatively, just as with the game, you can use physical representations of these business elements and assets by creating a tabletop map with moveable pieces. In the military, troops use rough versions of these all of the time and they are called sand tables.

If your business is not geographically based, create a map that is still based on visual representations of your Battlespace elements, but arrange them in a manner that is relevant to your operations. A flow chart type of display with assets, partners, and market conditions may be a good example.

Market

The market data should be placed on an additional overlay for ease of use and the ability to separate internal and external factors. What your market data includes will depend, again, on your industry and scope. If you own a convenience store, this would include all of the other convenience stores in proximity to yours. If you sell gas at your convenience store, it might include what prices the other stores are selling gas for. For the same type of business, including traffic counts on nearby roads might be important.

The market is not just your customers and their demand. It's also your competitors. The market is comprised of the positive and negative pressures that affect your operations. Going back to the real estate example, we did not include competitors in the sense of other companies doing the same thing we are. That doesn't matter to us. Our competition, in the end, is every other house being sold in the marketplace we are operating in. It doesn't matter if it's being sold by an investor or a homeowner- it's competing for buyer's dollars.

If you are a retailer, market data may include the number of products you have received orders for, placed on your map in the geo-location that they must be delivered to. Now, since you already plotted your factories or suppliers, you can start to visualize where your resources are and where they need to be applied.

Temporal

If your business operations are time sensitive, it makes sense to include a representation of time as a resource. This can be a challenge for some, but don't get wrapped around the axle with it. If your business is time sensitive, a factory that employs Just-in-Time material management for example, you and your team should have a firm enough grasp of the requirements to create a visual representation of it.

If you have difficulty applying a temporal aspect to your battle space, take a hard look at whether or not your business is, in fact, time sensitive. It might feel like it is to you, but if you can't apply it to your Battlespace model, it may be less important than you think.

About the only pitfall I see people fall into with Battlespace mapping is viewing their map as a plan. It is not a plan, it is a tool to help you plan and make decisions. What I mean by that, and in keeping with difficulties applying a temporal aspect, is if you are attempting to forecast something with your map, say when you will have enough money to pay off your warehouses, you are using it as a plan. If you use it to identify surfaces and gaps, opportunity and negative pressure, efficient distribution of assets and resources- you are using it as a tool for planning and decision making.

Other Elements

Your Battlespace should be coming together and you should already start to see how this is such an amazing and easy tool. What you add to your Battlespace is up to you, but I suggest you err on the side of adding too much. If you don't use the information, remove it. That's much better than getting into a planning process and wishing you had additional information represented. You can always add more, but you'll have to stop your train and shift gears to gather and add the information. If you've ever been interrupted while deep in thought, you know it can de-rail your movement forward.

There are any number of other elements you may need to add and these requirements will change over time. How quickly they change will depend on your planning horizon or decision horizon. For example, a company like UPS requires constant meteorological data to continue operating as efficiently as possible. Of course, they have sophisticated systems that track, report, and adjust for meteorological events- shifting routes, vehicles, and people very effectively.

Their system is much more technologically advanced, but it is absolutely no different than what we are describing here; it is a Battlespace map.

Chapter 3

Taking Risks Versus Making Gambles

If you've completed your map, or at least started it, there's a real possibility you are already seeing some advantages, opportunities, or untapped efficiencies. Personally, when I create a Battlespace map for my own businesses, or those of others, I see an immediate increase in clarity and even solutions to issues at hand.

So we're done, right? Not so much. The reality is that an inordinate number of businesses, both startups and well-established enterprises, fail every year. One might argue that there are a myriad of situations that result in a business failure. But the true reality is that these failures can almost always be traced back to two fundamental and very basic causes—the failure to create a sound, workable, and adaptable plan, and the consistent practice of not executing that plan correctly.

Now that you have defined your Battlespace and populated it with relevant elements, it's time to create a plan. Even if you created your Battlespace with a specific issue in mind, and can see a solution, don't forgo the following process. Admittedly, I will sometimes want to jump right to execution if an issue's solution is revealed through creating or manipulating the Battlespace map. I don't though, because there is value in planning. And, as you'll find, experience with this system will allow you to compress the process immensely for situations where extensive planning is not required. Where, initially, you may find it takes some investment of time to complete the process, you'll discover even a compressed process that takes just a few minutes will yield exponentially valuable results.

Before we get into the meat of the 5P, though, we need to cover a distinction between taking risks and making gambles. Even well formulated plans contain risk, it's a part of doing business. Plans built around gambles, though, rarely succeed and if they do it's more by luck than anything else. As leaders, we take risks, but we don't gamble with our businesses.

Decision Making: Risking Vs. Gambling

We all make decisions every day and your Battlespace map is the first tool in helping you make better ones, but there's more to it, of course.

Sometimes the decisions we make are simple; sometimes they are complex. Some decisions are routine and have little impact; some are critical and can create the conditions for winning or losing. Sometimes, we will have an extended amount of time to make our decisions and at others we will have to do so in split seconds. There are occasions where we will have a large volume of high quality information and intelligence on which to base our decisions. Most of the time, however, we will not have all of the information necessary to completely piece together the puzzle before us. It's at these times that risk takers are sorted from the gamblers.

Critical decision-making

If you look in the dictionary, you'll find "Decision" is similarly defined as "A conclusion or resolution reached after consideration." In practical terms, that means making choices between certain options. It's taking a direction and, therefore necessarily, not taking another.
In a greater sense, though, it's the basis for setting a series of yet to be known events into motion. Our decisions not only affect the immediate situation, but just as dominoes fall in series, our choices, and the actions that stem from them, have an impact into the future.

In military operations, critical decisions often mean the difference between life and death as well as success and failure. Interestingly, life and success are not mutually dependent in the military world. A commander may have to make a decision that will cause the death of troops, but ultimately achieve success by securing the objective.

As the level of command gets closer to direct combat, the time sensitivity typically elevates and decisions must be made in an instant. An example of this would be the difference between the time sensitivity of decisions made by the President and a fire team leader engaged in a firefight. The President's decisions will be funneled down to the forces and executed-this takes time. The fire team leader will make moment-to-moment decisions that will ultimately decide the fate of his team and the success of their mission. Certainly, there are occasions where higher echelon commanders make decisions that instantly impact tactical operations, but to illustrate our point, this example is effective.

The same holds true for business. For example, there is, and should be, a difference in the time sensitivity and decision impact of a large organizations CEO and customer service representative. A majority of the CEO's decisions should be strategic in nature; his or her decisions will be translated into tactics as they flow down the organization. They will have lower time sensitivity and the impact of their decisions will be great upon the organization. Their decisions will also have an extended time to impact. Meaning, whatever policies and directions they set will not be felt by the customer milliseconds after they are conveyed.

The customer service representative on the other hand will make tactical decisions as they work with customers. Their actions will directly impact the customer's sentiment and buying decisions. Their time sensitivity is typically very high and their time horizon is very short- as in through the end of their interaction with that customer (more on time horizon in a moment). The impact of their decisions is clear and immediate- the customer is either happy or they are not. The impacts their individual decisions make on the organization as a whole are generally undetectable. The collective impact of all of their decisions and how they affect the customers they interact with, however, is very important to the organization.

For the CEO, many of his or her decisions are critical to the success and longevity of the organization. Organizational leaders, managers, employees, investors, and most importantly, customers can feel the impact.

The customer service representative's decisions are critical to the satisfaction of the customer and collectively to the success of the organization. Unlike the CEO, however, their decisions are not felt so directly in an upward manner. If a customer service representative fails to take action that creates a happy customer, the CEO is unlikely to hear about it- unless it is of grave proportion or has created an immense liability. Most likely, the failure will go no further than the representatives' management.

Both share a need for having the ability, skill, and authority to make critical decisions relative to their positions. The ability is that of being able to be decisive- to make the decisions to apply a course of action that will lead to the desired outcome. The skill is in recognizing the issues and choosing the proper course of action. The authority is just that- being granted the power to act.

The ability to be decisive is relative. A CEO must be able to make decisions that have wide implications to the business; they will affect all of the stakeholders. The representative must be able to make decisions that represent the organization favorably towards the customer. They will affect that person's opinion and buying decisions. Both have a desired outcome- for the CEO, broadly, it's the success of the organization; for the representative it's the satisfaction of a customer.

In order to achieve a desired outcome, one must be established and understood. This is certainly a much more difficult task for the CEO as he or she is creating a vision for the entire organization. The concept is no less important at the representative's level though. If they do not understand what the desired outcome should be, then they will not be able to achieve it- except by luck. For this reason, if we expect our people to achieve an end result, we must tell them what that end result is. We must clearly articulate what we want to happen (we'll cover how to do that too).

The skill to recognize the issues and apply the proper course of action is also relative. A CEO must be able to recognize complex financial, marketing, and staffing issues. They must also be able to formulate and apply the correct course of action drawing from their experience and knowledge. The representative must be able to recognize what the customers' issues are- typically this can be achieved by listening and relating how they wish they were treated. They then must be able to choose the correct course of action. Generally, although there should be some room for creativity, the authority they have been granted will define these courses of action.

Depending on the products and services being rendered, the course of action chosen may be simple or complex, creative or quite standard. If a customer calls in with a complaint about a pair of shoes, they will probably be quite happy to receive a replacement pair free of charge.
If a customer calls in having received the wrong party favors for their only daughters wedding, which happens to be the next day, just sending new ones will not suffice. This is where the authority to act comes into play.

It should be obvious what the CEO's authority is- they're the CEO. For most organizations, what the customer service representative's authority is might not be and if it is, it is probably too restrictive. An example might be that an organization instructs their representatives that when a customer calls in about their shoes, they have the authority to process a replacement using a standard order replacement process.

If a customer calls in about their running shoes arriving and not fitting properly, but has a race the next day and they have been training for over a year- a replacement would not arrive in time. Granted, the customer may have ordered the wrong size and they shouldn't be running a race in a new pair of shoes, but those things aside- if they don't have their brand new shiny pair of running shoes, you're company will have an unhappy customer.

What if the representative had a budget to do things to make customers happy in extraordinary situations and in extraordinary ways? Perhaps that representative calls a retailer near the customer and arranges for them to fit her with a new pair of shoes that afternoon. Then, the representative sends the store a replacement pair. The customer feels like royalty, the store may gain a customer, and boy will that customer talk your company up at the race.

Nordstrom's is a great example for this. Their representatives know what the desired outcome is: make customers happy. That might seem too broad, but with the proper skills and authority, it's actually the exact opposite- it's very specific. It doesn't matter what problem you have with a product you purchased from Nordstrom's. If you're not happy, they fix it. It doesn't matter if it's old, broken, worn, or used on Noah's Ark as a bird's nest. If you bring it in, mail it in, send it by carrier pigeon, or hire the Hobbit to hand deliver it, they will replace it with a product you are happy with. Trust me on those, my wife enjoys finding the limits of their service and she hasn't yet been able too.

The skill comes into play with training and development. If a customer brings back a pair of shoes, instead of simply exchanging the shoes for the Identical pair, the representatives explore what it is about the shoe that is disliked. Perhaps they recommend a different style, size, or brand. They look for what will make the customer most happy.

The authority is quite simple in this case: every representative has the authority to make it right with product of equal value. With a quick phone call, they gain the authority to go beyond that by doing things like expedited shipping, pulling from other store inventories, etc. It is a model of customer service and what Nordstrom's is known for.

Information Extends Your Time Horizon

Time horizons are generally referred to as defined periods of time used for evaluation or simulation. In that form, they allow multiple factors or scenarios to be evaluated over the same term.

They are also used for traditional planning purposes, i.e. 1 year plan, 5 year plan, etc. In decision-making and strategic thinking, the time horizon takes on a different meaning and that's what we refer to here and throughout this book. Your time horizon is that point in the future when you are no longer able to accurately plan your actions because the information you currently have does not allow you to create a picture of what the operating conditions will be.

For example, you are creating a financial plan to pay your taxes into the future. You know there will be a change in the IRS code that will directly impact your industry in 12 months. You do not know what that change is, exactly, but you know it will drastically affect your financial plan. Now, we all know the IRS code never changes and when it does, it's as clear as the Caribbean Sea. But, just for a moment, lets assume that's not the case- I know it's a stretch. In this case, your time horizon for your financial plan is 12 months. After that point, you do not have the information you need to make accurate assumptions or decisions.

For the CEO, there are multiple time horizons that layer on top of one another. Certain business functions will have horizons that reach decades into the future and others, at times, may be less than 24 hours. The only way to extend your time horizons is with information. At best, you will have been able to refine your information into intelligence. (Information is raw data and intelligence is refined and actionable.) That won't always be the case though and raw information still extends your time horizon.

Picture yourself in a forest at night. It's so dark you can't see beyond your outstretched hand. Your time horizon extends out to your fingertips, about a half second in time or so. You can only act and react to events that occur after they pass within that reach. You take out a flashlight and turn it on. You can now see several meters in front of you clearly, but beyond that, the light begins to fade and you eventually lose all visibility.

The light is like information. The bright, clear light that allows you to see clearly is intelligence. The dimmer, fading light is information that has not been refined. The less refined it is, the less clear things are. Typically, this spatial representation of fading light is also true for information and time. The further out in time the information is, the less clearly it illuminates the space and the less actionable it is.

Some might say, "but, I know my competitor is planning on launching a device that does X,Y,Z 24 months from now." Okay, sounds like good information and it should shine like a spotlight. Wrong. Although that may be a brighter spot of information, it's 24 months out.

How many events will occur between now and then that will change your competitor's plan? Will you or someone else take action that makes that information irrelevant? Will consumers love it or hate it? There are too many variables for that information to be like a giant lighthouse on a rocky shore. Over time, you may refine it and make it intelligence, which would more clearly extend your time horizon.

From the front line to the CEO, the further out our time horizon is the better decisions we are able to make. In keeping with our example of the representative and shoes, if the customer disliked the product because the cut didn't fit them properly, they might leave with a new pair and return again next week a bit unhappier. By gathering information about why the customer disliked the shoes, the representative's time horizon is extended. They can make decisions about the future of the customer based on the information they have. Through a dialogue, they discover the shoe's form just isn't right for the customer's foot. So, they recommend an alternative that is more suited to their anatomy and that the customer likes with respect to style. The representative's extended time horizon allowed them to see that the same shoe would not make the customer happy. Now, the customer leaves happy and stays happy.

The Quality of Decisions

The quality of decisions we make is directly related to the quality of information we have. Note, I did not say quantity of information. If I was making an investment decision based on a company's financial health and had all of the financials in front of me, it wouldn't help me if the information were old or incorrect. The same is true for any decision we make. If one of your associates tells you they heard you are getting a promotion and huge raise and you go on a spending spree, that's probably not a quality decision based on quality information. If your boss calls you into his office and hands you a signed contract for a promotion and huge raise and you go on a spending spree, that's probably still not a quality decision, but at least it was based on quality information.

In a perfect world, we would have all of the best information available to us all the time. We would be able to base our decisions on hard facts, without ambiguity or risk. Well, it's not a perfect world. Every bit of information we have is either flawed or potentially flawed. Yes, every bit.

If we are dealing with raw numbers, they are information. How can raw numbers be flawed or have the potential to be flawed?

Well, how were they captured? Is it a result of human calculation? Who created the methodology for capturing and recording? Who created the formulas, parameters, and system? Someone had to and the question is, did they get it right? If a human played any part at all in the gathering of the data, it has a potential to be flawed. Miscalculations, errors in formulas, skewed parameters, and even motivations all affect the data, even numbers, we receive.

Take it a step further and consider the information you receive from reports and analysis. Someone had to do that too. Did they do it correctly? What are their past experiences that brought them to the conclusions they reached? What assumptions were made? These are all things that need to be considered.

I'm not by any means saying you can't trust any of the information you have at your disposal. I'm also not saying you need to evaluate the source of every single bit and byte that cross your desk. That would quickly lead to analysis paralysis. You have to have some level of trust that the information you are receiving is good and you have to dig deeper on the information you deem critical or possibly flawed. The point I am making is that we will never have all of the information we need to make every decision with absolute certainty that it's correct. This is where leadership comes in.

Uncertainty

Leaders must have the ability to make decisions in the face of uncertainty. They must be able to take the information available to them, process it, and conclude what course of action is best for the organization. If we wait until we have the best information available, we'll watch as our competitor's blow by us and customers flock away.

If the military only acted on absolutely perfect intelligence, there would be no action because perfect intelligence doesn't exist. Now, we would hope large-scale actions are based on pretty good intelligence, but even then the definition of "good" is open for debate.

This is by no means an easy task. If you've ever been in a leadership position, you've been faced with making a decision where you said to yourself, "If I only knew 'X' I could be sure." This is especially true when you're faced with a "this or that" decision. You have to choose one thing over the other, but you don't know what the consequences of either are. If you knew what the consequences of choosing just one of the options were, you would be able to make a brilliant decision between the two.

Unfortunately, as leaders, we are faced with those types of decisions everyday. We have to act based on our vision, experience, knowledge, organizational resources and capabilities, and whatever quality information we have. It's part of being a leader.

Risking vs. Gambling

There is a fine line between being a risk taker and a gambler. Leaders take risks and gamblers, well gamble. What's the difference?
When you take a risk, you are basing your decision on those things we mentioned above: our vision, experience, knowledge, organizational resources and capabilities, and quality information. When you take a risk, you have weighed the consequences and probability of failure (being wrong) with the rewards of being right. You've come to the conscience conclusion that you are going to take action in light of a possibly negative outcome and you've created mitigating factors to minimize both the probability of failure and the effect if it does occur.

When you gamble, you are simply taking a chance. You are not basing your decisions on experience, knowledge, resources, and quality information. You are basing your decision solely on the possibility of reward- often without proper consideration for the consequences of failure. Someone once said that I was wrong on this because professional gamblers do those things- they use their experience, knowledge, and weigh their available resources (money). Yes, completely true. But, "professional gamblers" aren't gamblers at all. They are professional risk takers. Ask a "professional gambler" what they do for a living and the real pro's won't tell you they're gamblers. They'll tell you they are a "professional poker player" or "professional blackjack player." Gamblers win once in a while, and it might be big, but risk takers win on purpose and, when they do lose, they recognize it quickly and take action.

Chapter 4

The 5 Paragraph Plan (5P)

The Marine Corps Planning Process (MCPP) and the Warriors Group Planning Process (WGPP) are top down processes. The planning and subsequent direction can be initiated at any level, but will flow down the organizational chain. Because of that, you might think it's best to start with the full WGPP and work down to the end user product, the 5P. It's not.

We would all probably agree that the Marine Corps is very effective at training Marines. When Marines are introduced to the military parent of this process, they are first taught the 5 Paragraph Order. There are a couple of reasons for that.

First, a new lieutenant or young Marine doesn't have a need to understand the full process. They have a need to take the direction of their seniors and to do so in a format that allows them to fully execute the intent of the commander issuing the order.

Second, without understanding the end user product first, it is difficult to conduct a planning process and achieve the results necessary to give the lower level commanders the information and direction they need in order to be able to execute. That's not to say the planning process is restricted by the end product, rather that an individual intimately familiar with the use of the 5 Paragraph Order is much more capable of guiding the planning process to a successful and comprehensive result. Conversely, a lack of that understanding can result in a need to reengage in the full planning process to satisfy lower level information requirements. Marines are taught the MCPP at a level commensurate with their role. It is a top down process taught from the bottom up.

I was once told there are two entities you can't argue with: God and the Marine Corps. I would probably personally add wives and mothers, but that's just me. I wouldn't necessarily agree that one can't argue with the Corps. In fact, the Corps relies on thinking men and woman more than most realize. In this case, though, I think their approach to teaching a planning process is spot on.

There are other reasons that apply to business. There are occasions in organizations, regardless of size, where simply using the 5P as both the planning and communication tool are appropriate. This could be because of the scope of the task or issue at hand. It could also be because a solution has already been identified and the course of action simply needs to be effectively conveyed. There are also organizations that may not require full engagement in the planning process solely based on their scope of operations, size, or both. An example of that would be a very small business, either in number of employees or business reach.

A sole proprietor and sole employee can certainly benefit from a full WGPP evolution, but the reality is that it probably isn't necessary every day, week, or even month. By completing the 5P component of the system, you will gain the insight, clarity, and executable plans necessary to increase your propensity to succeed. As your business grows, you can easily add higher-level elements to the system and seamlessly scale the process to your business. It's also true that a smaller business owner/manager tends to make decisions based on a small amount of inputs, which are easily managed in the 5P.

So, we start from the bottom up and learn the 5P. Then we will add higher-level elements of the WGPP. After you have become familiar with the 5P, used it, and read further, you'll find you inherently and necessarily employ some of the aspects of the higher-level elements in a less formal manner. It's no coincidence that it's built that way; it's a progressive system.

As a rule of thumb, if you are using the 5P as a planning and communication tool and find it is not comprehensive enough to satisfy the issue at hand, step up a level and employ the next higher process element.

Modes of Planning

Maneuver Management divides planning into three modes, based on the level of uncertainty surrounding the plan. The three modes are Active, Contingency, and Possibility.

Active planning occurs when we are reasonably confident in our forecasts of the future. In this case, we can formulate a specific plan and apply actual resources. Active planning is what most people think of when they think of planning and we do it all of the time in all of our activities. Think about the process you go through to simply mow the lawn. You might think, I need gas, bags for the clippings, etc. You might reason, I need to wait until the dew dries and then get started before the day gets too hot. This is active planning.

Contingency planning occurs when there is sufficient uncertainty about the future to preclude a commitment to one specific plan of action. As long as we have a reasonably good idea about the possibilities, we create a contingency plan. In this mode, we address several different possible scenarios, and define—generally in broad terms—what we would do in each case.

This mode gives us the flexibility to adapt to a changing environment, and to respond quickly as situations requiring actions arise. We lay the groundwork for future actions as the events we are planning for begin to unfold. We balance our level of preparation with the flexibility necessary for an uncertain future.

Possibility planning is reserved for those times when our level of uncertainty is so high that it we are unable to create contingencies. In this mode, we don't define a specific set of actions so much as assessing the situation from a broad perspective for the purpose of building situational awareness.

We seek to gain an understanding of what the possible situation is so that we can respond to a broad range of circumstances, if and when they occur. This allows us to be somewhat prepared, while remaining flexible.

I should also point out that the modes of planning could also represent a sequential planning process. When you are first confronted with a situation or potential scenario, you begin an assessment of it—Possibility Planning.

As events begin to unfold, you begin to determine possible courses of action—Contingency Planning. And when the fog of uncertainty begins to clear and a likely situation presents itself, you begin to map resources and actions to the situation— Active Planning.

Smaller businesses may not see a need for planning beyond Active Planning. Many are operating on the edge all the time and are either completely reactive or barely proactive. I would argue that you do have a need for Possibility and Contingency Planning. In fact, I would wager you already do it at some level, even if not consciously.

Possibility planning, in particular, may seem irrelevant, especially for smaller businesses. The fact is that it significantly reduces the time required to react to changes in the Battlespace and that time savings could mean the difference between winning and losing against your competition.

Consider how many times you have heard rumor of a potential change in the market- a new competitor, Walmart coming to town, a government relocation or tax change. Did you think about how that would affect you and what you might do if it occurred? If you did, you engaged in very informal Possibility or Contingency Planning.

You might not have a need to make that a formal process. In some of my businesses, our Possibility Planning is as simple as a 30-minute staff meeting where we create a common situational awareness and record our discussions on the matter. Some of our Contingency Planning consists of a conference call where we weigh certain options against our resource availability to ensure alignment if certain events occur. A key element in making these modes of planning informal and still effective is to record your thoughts, ideas, concerns, etc. You may need to come back to them at a later date- don't expect yourself to remember everything you considered or thought. I know my mind is constantly turning and if I don't record (write, voice memo, etc.) that type of information, it will likely be lost into the ether. Not only will you have to spend time and energy on re-thinking what you've already found, but great ideas will be lost.

Other businesses of mine have very formal Orientation and Contingency Planning sessions. It all depends on the business, events being considered, and complexity of the organization. Do what works for you, but do it.

Leaders Intent

There's one last item we need to cover before I introduce you to the 5P. Maneuver Management, as you will see, is more than just a system to plan and communicate. It's more than a way to think about your business and strategy, more than a way to create order from near chaos. Maneuver Management will help you empower your organization to execute your plans and work towards your vision.

In order to do that, we need to effectively convey what that vision is. Specifically, what your vision is for the execution of the plan on the table. Depending on the level of your plan, it could be a vision for the future of the company as a whole or it could only pertain to the accomplishment of the mission your plan addresses.

When you arm your organization with your vision, you empower them to use their own best judgment, initiative, and creativity to achieve the end result you desire. You remove the need to micro-manage every person and every task. Your employees will appreciate this and if you have the right people on board, they will surprise you with their ingenuity. Consider the possibility that the people in your organization may know how to get you to where you want to be better than you do. It's not always the case, but it's a real possibility and you'll always be stuck in the same routine unless you empower your people to get the job done. If you don't have the right people on board, you'll find out quickly and can either train them up or replace them.

Empowering the people in your organization to make decisions and take action is called decentralizing. It's important to note that you can decentralize the authority to make decisions and take action, but you cannot pass on the responsibility of the end results to anyone. You are ultimately responsible for what you and your people do or fail to do.

Decentralizing is a key tenant in Maneuver Management. The bad news is that it's a scary proposition for many, especially small business owners. The good news is fourfold: you don't have to do it all at once, take small steps; it's easy to recentralize if you need to; the rewards of a decentralized organization are many; and Maneuver Management will help you get there.

In Maneuver Management, the leaders grand vision for the end state of the plan is called Leaders Intent. It's not called vision because the word carries certain connotations with it that elude to it being a general concept of what you would like to see happen. Leaders Intent is not general.

Your Leaders Intent is a specific statement about what the end state of executing your plan is. A good example is, "By COB of the third shift on 14 July, the line is ready for the contractors. By COB of the third shift on 16 July, all personnel have received the required training and are ready to return to the line on the 17th. By COB of the first shift on the 17th, we are running at standard capacity." (The complete 5P example surrounding this example can be found in the resources section of The Warriors Group website www.TheWarriorsGroup.com).

The 5P

The complete Marine Corps 5 Paragraph order is somewhat of a misnomer because it includes a lot more than 5 paragraphs. Each of the 5 main sections often includes sub sections and sub-sub sections. Higher-level orders can exceed thousands of pages. We've included a complete breakdown of the actual USMC 5 Paragraph order in the Resources section of our website, but rest easy, the 5P is a streamlined approach refined over years of real world business use and it can be less than a page or as long as you need it to be.

The 5P has a predefined structure. In theory, it's as simple as populating the plan with the relevant information, as defined below. Remember that it's not the length of the plan that's important; it's what the plan conveys. Steer away from verbosity and focus on efficient brevity. Check out the Warriors Group website Resource section, to see specific examples of simple completed plans.

So, one last time, let's be clear, the 5P is both a planning tool and a method of communication. It's a planning tool because you can use it to identify information you require, things you need to consider, and so on. For instance, if you begin by populating the 5P, you will inevitably have sections that you cannot complete without further information and/or planning—these are your planning needs.

It is the most effective method for communicating your plan because it allows your entire organization to plan and execute within a standard format. It also clearly, concisely, and systematically conveys all the information necessary for your organization to execute the plan or engage the planning process at their level.

One of the most often experienced traps with business planning is not starting. That is, an individual or group sits down with the full intent of putting together a plan, but never get past the starting line. That's because they don't know where to start. The 5P alleviates that by giving you a structure in which to initiate and conduct your planning.

At the higher levels of the WGPP, the answers to the questions needed to create a comprehensive plan are discovered. As I said though, it's not always necessary to engage at that level. As you work within the Maneuver Management system, you'll get better at developing the information and direction needed for the 5P. To help you get started, I have put together a list of questions you can use to jumpstart the process of writing a 5P.   You'll find it in the resource section of The Warriors Group Website as well.

With that, meet the 5P.

1. SITUATION
a. <u>General</u>—Describe the overall framework of the plan itself, and the conditions that have led to the creation of it. For example, you would include the reasons why the plan is necessary and the process that has led up to the creation of the plan.

b. <u>Battlespace</u>—This describes the competitive landscape where your plan will be deployed. Alternatively, if the plan is strictly internal, describe the operating environment where the plan will be carried out. Ideally, you have an actual Battlespace map and this section elaborates on the conditions set forth visually on the map.

c. <u>Competition / Obstacles</u>—If the plan is dependent on any interaction with outside competitors, they should be identified in this section, along with an explanation of their impact. Alternatively, if the plan is strictly an internal initiative, any issues or forces that might impede the plan should be identified as well.

d. <u>Partners / Leverage</u>—If the plan integrates with any external companies who share a mutual interest in seeing the initiative succeed, they should be identified, along with their interest. If the plan is strictly internally facing but there are forces or issues that might help the plan to succeed, they should be identified here as well. Interdepartmental initiatives would indicate partnering departments.

2. MISSION
The plan's mission statement should be a concise and succinct explanation of the plan's purpose, an overview of the tasks that will be implemented, and most importantly the goal that will be achieved. The mission statement should provide the basic who, what, when, where, how and why for the plan. Think of the mission statement as the plan's "Executive Summary."

3. EXECUTION
Whereas the Mission paragraph was an overall summary, the Execution paragraph is the detail.

a. <u>Leaders Intent</u>—We talked about Leaders Intent above. The Leaders Intent explains the vision of the planners in terms of desired outcomes, and sets forth a framework for accomplishing those outcomes. It is intended to provide sufficient guidance to complete the mission, while allowing sufficient latitude to operate with flexibility and initiative.

b. <u>Concept of Operations</u>—If necessary, the Concept of Operations section explains how all of the moving parts of the plan will work together.

c. Tasks—This section contains a detailed and granular list of tasks that need to be completed in order to achieve the stated goal and to complete the mission. The task lists should be organized by responsible party, and in order of timing and importance. Task lists should be calendar driven.
d. Coordinating Instructions—If the plan calls for the creation of a cross functional team within the organization, this section should detail how they are to work together.

4. ADMINISTRATION AND LOGISTICS
a. Costs—This is the budget for the plan. Each task should be listed, along with its respective cost. Depending on the organization, budget roll ups might be prepared by department or functional business area as well.
b. Personnel—This section should list all personnel who are working on the project as well as their respective roles. In the case of a large organization where a diverse cross functional team has been created, this section can also provide biographical information so team members can gain an appreciation of who they are working with.
c. Logistics—This section explains the deployment of organizational resources anticipated in support of the plan. Any coordination issues that relate to these resources should also be addressed here. Additionally, if resources must be moved from one location to another, or if travel is required for personnel, the details should be spelled out here.

5. MANAGEMENT
a. Personnel Responsibilities—For large and complex plans, it is often useful to detail the broader responsibilities that individuals will perform. In this regard, the Personnel Responsibility section serves as a mini-job description by defining the broader aspects of personal roles.
b. Chain of Command—The project chain of command details the reporting structure for the plan itself. It is usually sufficient to detail this structure in a graphical format that is essentially an organizational chart developed specifically for the implementation of the plan.
c. Reporting—The reporting section details how the project team members will report up the chain of command. This section should detail the metrics that will be measured, along with reporting formats and timetables. This is a critical component of the overall planning process since the only way the plan can be managed properly is if the correct metrics have been identified and measured.

It's important to once again note that the lower the plan travels down through the organization, the less broad it becomes. An example of this is that a CEO level 5P will most likely not include specific budget details. Instead, one of the tasking's in the CEO's plan would be for the appropriate leaders at the appropriate levels to define the budget in accordance with any restraints and directives issued in the plan.

The key to success in using the 5P is to stay focused on what you are planning to do and the level of detail necessary to plan properly at your level.

This part is critical—do not become bogged down by attempting to micro-manage the details or dictate the tactics unless you are at the level of tactical execution. Empower your people to make these decisions and trust that they will make good ones. By the way, this is all part of the learning and development process. Remember, Leaders Intent applies to anyone who has someone working for him or her.

Now is a good time to stop and create a 5P of your own. Use the template I provide and the resource section at The Warriors Group Website (www.TheWarriorsGroup.com). Start with a simple plan, it could be as basic as planning a family event for the weekend or a trip to the grocery store. This is just to get your feet wet with the 5P; I don't expect you'll be issuing a 5P to your family. Although, I'd be lying if I said I had never done that. I think it's important to start with a very simple plan in order to get comfortable with the 5P and see the power the tool has. I don't want you to try to tackle a major issue right from the start, because grasping the simplicity of the 5P, regardless of the scope of the plan, is very important for moving forward.

Next, it's time to learn how to succeed using the 5P in the Leadership Success Model and the rest of Level II.

LEVEL II

Chapter 5

The Leadership Success Model

Success doesn't just happen. Certainly, for some it comes easier than others. At the core though, there are a few things successful people have in common. Not every successful person has all of these things, but there are some that are required. There aren't any secrets to success. It comes down to great ideas and great leadership.

In the following pages, I am going to explain the Leadership Success Model. This is a representation of the most efficient process for creating and sustaining success. Again, no secrets will be divulged here- they don't exist. What does exist is a methodology for creating success that works. It will only work for you, though, if you work at it.

You will have to learn some lessons along the way. You might even fail before you get it right. Take heart- most of the worlds greatest success stories have big failures in their history. Sometimes, failures can be more valuable than successes- so long as you learn from them and apply those lessons to your next endeavor. If you give up or fail to recognize why you failed then you are simply a failure. Instead, when you fail, use it to be a success story that earned it.

Success is not defined in a singular form. For some, it's dominating an industry. For others, it might be improving the way a department is run. Success is scalable relative to what you are trying to achieve.
We'll talk more about that in a minute, but it's important to understand that success isn't always being at the top of a market or becoming a household name; sometimes its as simple as achieving what you set out to do.

The Idea

All successful people have this in common. I am calling it "The Idea" and it includes products, concepts, direction for an organization, a goal, or whatever it is that you believe will change the terms of the status quo and lead to success. To over simplify it a bit, it could be filling your pantry with all the food you need for a month instead of going to the store every week.

Without "The Idea," you have nowhere to go. If you simply want to be successful, but have no vehicle for achieving that, you will remain in your current situation. You need "The Idea."

Perhaps you have a product in your mind that you believe will rival the iPhone. Perhaps it's not such a game changer, but you believe there is a great demand for it. Maybe you see a function your organization is not providing, but that consumers really want. It could even be changing the way your organization functions internally. Frankly, it could even be changing your health and deciding to run a marathon. Whatever it is, it's "The Idea" and it's the basis for going forward. It's the reason we will engage in the Leadership Success Model. It is the means to our success.

"The Idea" must be clearly defined. Saying you will change the way your department functions and stopping there is not "The Idea." That is a desire. Saying you will change the way your department functions by developing and implementing a software based tracking system is "The Idea."

Like wise, saying you will get healthy is a desire. Saying you will get healthy by registering, training for, and completing a marathon is "The Idea."

If you lack "The Idea," you will probably need the full Warriors Guide Planning Process, which we'll cover in later chapters.

The Endstate

All successful people have this in common as well. Some might call this "vision". It is the ability to create a picture of what a successful outcome looks like; it's a snapshot of the future. It's not just a loose mental picture; rather it is the definition of success relative to your endeavor. Keep it simple and don't get drawn into the trap of attempting to define how you are going to get there- not yet. If you do, you are likely to get mired down and discouraged by the details. We'll get there soon enough.

Lets continue our examples of improving a department and getting healthy. The Endstate for improving your department might be: The new software system has improved efficiency by 50% and the need for overtime has been eliminated; My employees are communicating effectively and interdepartmental request response time has been decreased to less than 24 hours; My department has become a model for the entire organization.

With getting healthy, it might be: My blood pressure has been reduced to125/85; I lost 25 pounds; I followed my training routine and completed the marathon as planned; I am continuing to run and improve the state of my health. If this looks a lot like Leaders Intent, that's because your Leaders Intent is derived from your desired Endstate.

Be specific, but keep it simple. That might sound oxy-moronic, but its not. Define what success looks like for this endeavor- not the rest of your career or life. Chances are you will want to build on your success- you should. It's fine to include a continuance, but not a definition of future Endstates. For example: "I am continuing to run and improve the state of my health." That's a bridge, not a new city. By including a continuance, or building a bridge, you are defining your success as also creating conditions favorable to further success. You are not defining your success by everything you do in the future.

It is possible to reverse engineer "The Idea" from The Endstate. In fact, for some, it's just the way they work. If you are one of those people, just be sure to develop your Endstate clearly enough to arrive at a starting point- "The Idea." Don't get caught in the trap of seeing your Endstate as "The Idea." Also, don't expect others to work that way. Don't expect them to buy in to your Endstate without "The Idea."

Idea/Endstate Agreement

Is this beginning to feel like a process? It is. Success is brought about by systematic action focused on getting there. All of that begins with "The Idea," but doesn't end there. We have to be disciplined in our approach and honest in our criticisms. We have to look for lessons and learn them well.

Now that we have established what "The Idea" is and what The Endstate looks like, its time to turn our focus to whether or not "The Idea" is a good one relative to The Endstate. First and foremost, with regards to this, is whether or not "The Idea" has the capability to create, through our actions, the desired Endstate. If your Endstate is to generate $1 Million a month in revenue, but your product price is $1 and you can only produce 1000 units a month, it's not going to work. We can see that without even knowing what demand will be.

If your revenue Endstate were the same, but your product price is $10,000 and you can produce 500 units a month, there is certainly agreement between your Idea and Endstate with regards to revenue- insofar as capacity/price goes.

We also have to ask whether "The Idea" will fill the results defined in the Endstate. For the departmental software example, is the software actually capable, if created and used properly, of facilitating the improvements in efficiency and communication. Is there agreement between what you want to see happen and what you are using to get there? If there is, great- press on. If not, then what's more important to you, "The Idea" or the Endstate? If it's the earlier, then consider adjusting your Endstate. If it's the latter, do you need a new "Idea" to get there?

Self Analysis

Not all successful people have to do this- at least not if they are happy with their current position. I would argue that at some point in their journey, all successful people have had to take this step though. After working through various endeavors, people will learn a lot about themselves: their will, their skills, and abilities. If they are operating within the same framework on future endeavors, they will have a relatively thorough understanding of what they are capable of.

This step is not a guarantee for success- none of these steps are. Many, including this one, can greatly reduce the probability of failure though. For this step specifically, that happens for a few reasons.

In a Self Analysis, we have to ask some questions relative to "The Idea" at hand and about ourselves in general. We are not asking about finances and resources just yet. Again, don't get mired down in the details of other elements. If you take this step by step and focus on the step at hand, you'll be able to appraise the endeavor clearly and intelligently. This step is just about you as a person.

Be courageous in your assessment- expect your best. Be realistic too. As a basic example, I know I am savvy with spreadsheets and can create some very useful tools, solve complex problems, etc. I also know that there is absolutely no way I can tackle Einstein's Relativity in Excel. We have to ask:

> Am I capable of seeing this through? That's a loaded question. It doesn't just ask whether you are willing to take this endeavor to task, here we ask whether you have the ability to lead yourself and others through to success.

> Do I have the skills and abilities necessary, be they physical, mental, technical, and even emotional? Be honest, it's critical.

Am I willing to make the sacrifices that may be necessary? This comes down to priorities. You might not be called on to make any sacrifices at all. You might find yourself embattled in office politics. Perhaps the endeavor will reduce the amount of time you have with your family. Weigh the price of success against the rewards. Not everything is worth doing and in doing some things you undo others. Is what you are contemplating embarking on worth the price of getting there?

Is this in line with my personal values? If you are considering doing something that is not aligned with your values then you are less likely to see it through if things get tough. You are also less likely to make good decisions because those decisions might call for you to act outside of your core values. Not all of these questions are deal killers and we'll discuss that shortly. This one, however, is. If you do not believe this endeavor fits with your values, don't do it. It's that simple. I'll tell you that the sacrifices you will make will not be worth the success. Those sacrifices will be deep and personal. We can't recover time- spend yours doing things you believe in and feel "right" about.

Am I passionate about this? Passion is key, but not always necessary. Yes, it's true. There are occasions where we need to succeed at things that don't fill our sails. These are the little things that lead to the big. The big deals though- The Big Ideas- must absolutely be backed by passion. There is, however, a twist. Ideally, your passion is for "The Idea;" you love the product or direction. Success can also be the passion. (For some people, their passion to succeed supersedes their passion for "The Idea.") That's okay so long as decisions about "The Idea" are not made in a fog of desire to be successful at all costs. Passion, in both respects, must be contained in order to act wisely. If you lack both passion for "The Idea" *and* passion for success- find another idea.

If you answered "no" to being capable as a leader, having the skills and abilities, making sacrifices, or having the passion (for "The Idea" or for success), your endeavor may not be over yet and we'll get to that.

If you answered "no" to being in line with your values or not having passion (for "The Idea" *and* success), go no further. Maybe you can sell your idea to someone or convince someone to champion it in your organization, but I wouldn't recommend doing it yourself. You are setting yourself up for failure. Yes, failure brings great lessons, but there is also a lesson in recognizing failure is the most likely outcome.

Resource Aggregation

In order to complete a comprehensive and accurate plan, you will need to know what resources you have at your disposal. You will need to identify all of the pertinent resources you have for this endeavor. They may include: human, facility, financial, material, technological, intellectual, legal, and many more.

The alignment or deficiency of your resource pool will be identified in the planning process. For now, you just need to know what resources you have. You are aggregating, not analyzing.

Create the Plan

It doesn't matter what "The Idea" is, you need a plan to make it happen. The level of planning you will need to engage in, the depth of your plan, and the time it takes to complete your plan will vary greatly depending on what you are endeavoring to do.

You've already learned the 5P and in future chapters you'll learn the WGPP. Both of these tools will work regardless of what your endeavor is. They are both completely scalable and are effective for everything from launching a new product in a multi-national company to scheduling a meeting and everything in between.

As mentioned above, if your Self Analysis yielded negative results, save value alignment and complete lack of passion, you may still be able to succeed. We explore that possibility through the planning process.

Necessarily, as you develop your plan, you will be required to apply your resources, including human resources. This is because you will need to identify whom you will assign tasks, roles, and responsibilities to. You will identify key players inside and outside of your organization.

If your Self Analysis showed you have a deficiency in skill or ability, do you have the human resources to fill that gap? If so, your Idea still has life. It's important to recognize the gravity of your decision to move forward with reliance on the core abilities or skills of another individual. You must have a clear understanding of what they are capable of, how they interact with your plan and other key players, what authority they require, and what the consequences are if they fail.

Remember, the ultimate success or failure of your endeavor remains with you. This is leadership, by the way. As your endeavors grow greater in scale, you will have to rely on the skills and abilities of others- you can't do everything yourself. Likewise, as you take on higher positions within an organization, you will have to employ your people to get the job done.

This is also the time to ensure alignment with your financial resources. Do you have the capital or funding to complete the endeavor? Depending on what you propose to do, that might mean fitting your Idea into your departments budget, financing development of a product, sustaining yourself and your family until revenue is being generated, or any other number of situations.

Along with human and financial, if you find a deficiency in other resources, can you fill those gaps? As you develop your plan using the WGPP and/or the 5P, you will identify roles, responsibilities, tasks, and needs. As you apply resources to those items it will become clear whether or not you are adequately sourced.

As you plan, do not build your initial plan around your resources. Create your ideal plan and then apply your resources. If you have a resource deficiency, decide if you can adjust your plan to your resources and still be effective or if you need to acquire more resources to meet your plan. This is a somewhat cyclical process. If you need to acquire more material resources, for example, you will need to revisit your financial resources to ensure continued alignment.

Create Metrics

Once you have completed the planning process and developed your plan, you will need to create metrics to track and evaluate the results of your plan execution. What data you need depends on what you are trying to achieve. You may need to track costs, website traffic, customer response, or efficiency. You may need to be able to measure response or shipping time. The possibilities are as broad as the number of variables in your plan.

When creating metrics, realize that every metric creates an administrative requirement. You will need to gather data, analyze the data, and output the data in a meaningful and useful form. You will also need to promulgate that information to applicable players.

Measure what you need to measure, track what you need to track, but don't create metrics simply for the benefit of having metrics. Give yourself and your people the information they need, in the form they need it, to accomplish the mission. Don't burden them with the task of gathering data and reporting on issues that don't have an impact or weigh them down with information they don't need.

Good metrics give you an indication of your position within the context of your plan. I liken this to navigating using your map to success. After the planning process, you will know where you are and where you want to go. You have a starting point and can plot your preferred destination. If you launch your plan and expect to get to the destination without referring to your map along the way, the probability of getting lost is very high. Metrics allow you to plot your position as you go. You may find you are following the shortest path or you may find you are out in the wilderness and need to make adjustments. In order to adjust correctly, you need to know your current position on the map.

As a leader, you may be in the position where you know what information you need to make decisions, but don't know how to track it, compile it, or output it in a format useful to you. Do you have the resources to assign those tasks to? If so, ensure your plan has that included. If not, can you acquire those resources? If you do not know how to analyze or apply the information you need to make decisions- learn it. You can have others track, compile, and output for you. As a leader, you must be able to understand that information and how it affects or applies to your plan. Leaders make decisions, adjust course, and affect change. Without the ability to interpret the information in your metrics, you are unable to do any of those things well.

Communicate the Plan

You have developed your plan and decided you have the resources to engage. Your resources are properly aligned and you have created metrics to plot your position along the way. Now, its time to get the troops engaged.

Depending on scale, your plan may only involve you. It may involve tens of thousands of people. You obviously have a need to communicate your plan if it involves you plus even one. Without clear, concise, and comprehensive communication of your plan, it will die a silent death.

It may not be so obvious that you should still communicate your plan even if it only involves you. There is great value in process of preparing your plan for communication. As you do so, you may discover gaps, additional tasking or needs, or even major flaws. Preparing your plan for communication forces you to step outside your plan just enough to gain, even slightly, an objective point of view.

Since you employed the WGPP and/or the 5P for your planning, this is a streamlined step. You will use the 5P for communicating the plan as well. We do this because it is a standardized and comprehensive format for conveying plan details, objectives, mission, and tasking at the appropriate level of detail to the appropriate people. It is also a coherent methodology that can be utilized at all levels of your organization. For those outside of your organization that might not be employing the 5 Paragraph tool, it is easily understood and clearly identifies tasks, roles, and responsibilities as well as the overall mission and objectives. It instantly integrates them into your plan by allowing all players to operate from a common plan picture.

Execute the Plan

Planning for the sake of planning might be a good exercise once in a while, but it won't get the job done. Executing a plan moves you from where you are now to somewhere else. Executing a plan well gets you there in a better way. Executing a plan that is well formulated, comprehensive, well communicated and understood, well- that gets you closer to where you intended to go and closer to success.

Don't let that point pass unnoticed. Execution quite simply means doing something. It means doing what you understand you are supposed to be doing to get to a certain result. Any action taken in that vain will inevitably change your position. Just because you do that, however, doesn't mean you will gain the results desired. If the plan is misunderstood or actions are flawed, the result will be a movement that is not necessarily in accord with the intention of the plan.
So, executing a plan, as it is understood, will move you, but not necessarily where you want to go. Executing the same well will get you there in a better way. Now, take a plan that explains the mission, objectives, tasks, roles, responsibilities, and Leaders Intent- a plan like that executed well will get you closer to where you want to go and in a better way.

Evaluate the Results

After execution begins, data for your metrics will likewise begin being collected. It's critical to evaluate your metrics. Again, your metrics allow you to plot your position on your map to success. We've all heard phrases like "If you don't know where you are going, how are you going to get there?" and "If you don't know where you are going, how will you know you've arrived?"

Similarly, if you don't know where you are, how are you going to get to where you want to go. That applies at the beginning of the planning process equally as much as it does during your execution phases. It's critical you know where you are on your map. Without that, adjustments will be missed or made in the dark. Executing a plan cannot be done in a vacuum. Internal and external factors will influence your plan from the moment you say, "go."

Perhaps equally as important as knowing where you are, is understanding why you got there. If you don't know that, you are likely to make the same mistakes, or miss reinforcing positive behavior, as you go forward.

If you find yourself traveling along the path at a great clip, just as planned, reinforce the behaviors being exhibited by you and your employees. Also, take lessons learned and apply them to improve performance and results. Be careful here though- there is a fine line between making improvements and implementing unnecessary changes.

Every time you implement a change to a tactic, strategy, process, or procedure that is working, you risk negatively impacting it instead of improving it. I see this all the time. Organizations see what they believe is an opportunity to improve performance. Perhaps an individual believes, although performance is good, it can be better. In many cases, that's true- in fact, in most cases even good or great performance can be improved upon.

The errors come from basing changes on faulty judgment, bad or missing information, wrong perceptions, lack of capability, or making changes that impede other functionalities. It's quite possible to increase performance in one function while negatively affecting others.

I am not saying that organizations and people should settle for "good." It should be a goal to continually improve performance, be the "best," and define the gold standard. That said, changes should be implemented based on validated information, actual capabilities, correct judgment and perceptions, and with the effects on other functions in full awareness. They should also be implemented at the correct time. If your organization is in the heat of battle and your people are at full capacity- implementing a tactical change that requires a great deal of resources from them (time, energy) probably isn't the best decision. For example, implementing a new Point of Sale system in a retail organization on Black Friday probably isn't wise.

The Marines have a saying, "Good initiative, bad judgment." That's saying it was great the individual took action, but the action was flawed. It could have been flawed because it was the wrong action or it was the right action executed at the wrong time and place. The lesson is to take initiative, but temper your desire to take action with good judgment.

If, in your evaluation, you find you are not even on the same map page, you'll need to find out why. Of course, there's a catch here too. You need to identify the cause, not the symptoms. Organizations pay consultants grand amounts of money to help them discover what the root causes of their issues are. Sometimes, it is necessary to bring in consultants- namely when your organization lacks the human resources with the necessary skills and experience to diagnose your illness or implement new programs, training, or technology. Having said that, I believe organizations turn to consultants too often. They don't realize they have the resources to organically solve their problems.

Consider the effects of your own people taking ownership of an issue or problem, creating solutions, and implementing those solutions. It creates cohesion in your organization. It creates a feeling of mutual vesting- the employee to the organization and vice versa. It increases the confidence of your employees and in your organization.

Identifying symptoms is relatively easy. Things like "Sales are down," "Customer loyalty is low," and "Employee turnover is high" are all symptoms. A symptom is simply how the pain is felt- just like a physical illness. When you go to the doctor, you don't say, "I have a hairline fracture in my fifth metatarsal." You say, "Hey Doc, my foot hurts."

Identifying the cause is more difficult. It's actually a way of thinking more than anything. When looking for the root cause of a symptom, you have to drill down until you reach the cause- it's what can't be broken down any further. Causes create the periodic table of business pain. They are the elements of what make businesses hurt.

Finding root causes is both a skill and ability. Everyone has the ability to think. Not everyone has the ability to think in an analytical manner that facilitates drilling down to the root of issues. The good news is that this can be taught to people who do have the ability to think analytically. It's also a skill derived from experience. If someone is looking for the cause of an issue, but does not know how the processes and functions of the organization interact, they will not be able to identify the cause-effect relationships necessary for a correct diagnosis.

As with other skills, this can most certainly be taught. Experience will refine this skill over time and use. I called the root causes of business issues the periodic table for two reasons. First, these are the elemental causes. For example, an organization feels like nothing is getting done. Nothing getting done is a symptom, not the cause. There are a lot of potential causes for this. By asking the right questions, we can drill down through the layers.

For this example, lets say we discover the employees are unclear about what their roles and responsibilities are; this is also still a symptom. We find the leadership knows what the employees' roles and responsibilities are, but are not communicating it. This might seem like the root cause: it's a failure to communicate. It might not be. Is there a method for communicating that includes clarity on roles and responsibilities? If not, the root cause is that the organization does not have a system for clear communication between leadership and employees. We would implement the 5P tool. If there is a system, we look at whether it is being used. If it is, then it is ineffective. If it is not, then we step back up one level and the root cause is in fact a leadership failure. Additionally, we would evaluate the current communication system to ensure it would work if used properly.

Second, all businesses share the same problems. Yes, your business and people are unique. Yes, your products and services have differentiation. No, you don't have problems that exist only in your organization. You may have technical issues that exist only in your business if you are the only company that provides a specific product, but your business problems are the same business problems other businesses have. The may taste a little different, but they're the same dish.

Just like the periodic table, every business problem can be listed in its elemental form. From these, all symptoms extend. That's where education and experience come into play. Teach your people what the root problems are and how to drill down to them. Then give them the experience gained only from working through real problems. You will build your own team of "consultants". Once you and your employees learn to look deeper, past the symptoms, identifying root causes will become second nature. At that point, you'll have the organic resources you need to succeed.

Adjustments

Once you have completed your evaluation and identified the root causes, you can create adjustments to your plan based on your findings. I remember being on the artillery range at The Basic School in Quantico Virginia. We were conducting a "FAMFIRE"- a familiarization fire – by calling in artillery fire. Each lieutenant was allocated 6 rounds. We were to demonstrate our understanding of the knowledge we gained in the classroom, about how to effectively call for artillery, by hitting a target a few thousand meters away on the range.

Each Lt. had an experienced artillery instructor helping us along. When it was my turn I spotted my target, plotted it on my map and felt I was pretty close to its location. I grabbed the radio and called for the first round- it hit about 100 meters too far. I felt I judged the distance I needed to adjust accurately and picked up the radio to make the adjustment and "fire for effect" (that's when you know you've got the target location and call for a barrage of artillery shells). My instructor stopped me and asked what my next move was. I quickly explained I was going to drop 100 yards and fire for effect. He advised against it saying that it was better to make a big adjustment, because our perception of distance at that range was distorted. So, I called in another spotting round 200 meters closer. Sure enough, it was 100 meters too short.

Surely, this was a great learning experience, because I learned that my ability to perceive distance was pretty good (being facetious). But, I wanted to get the biggest bang I could out of my 6 rounds. I wanted 5 rounds exploding in rapid succession right on my target. Now I had four. So, add 100 meters and fire for effect. I did well, but it wasn't the picture of destruction I had envisioned and I walked off the line kicking myself for not going with my gut.

Why am I telling you this story? Well there is a lesson there I have never forgotten. The advice was "make big adjustments," but my gut said I had it. The goal in pinning down the location of a target for artillery is called bracketing. If you're too far, drop some. If that's too short, split the difference and your close enough. Close doesn't only count in horseshoes and hand grenades- it counts in artillery too. That said, the Marines who spot and man the batteries can place an artillery shell through a basketball hoop from miles away- they are the best in the world at what they do.

There's something to be said for that as applied to business. There are issues where the exact target is difficult to discern.   You take a shot and miss, adjust your aim and fire again. Even if it takes a few adjustments, you'll be able to bracket the target and then focus fire on it. There's also something to be said for going with your gut. I knew I had it and should have gone for it. It was a little adjustment, but it was the right one.

If you really believe you've got the target pinned down, make the adjustment that will get effects on target. Don't make a big adjustment if its not warranted. Again, every adjustment has the potential to have negative effects, especially when it goes against your better judgment. If you know what you know, have confidence in it and make the call.

Cycle Back

Just like communicating your plan is critical to execution, communicating changes to your plan is also critical. After you have made decisions about what adjustments to make and where, you must communicate that to your organization. Nothing new here, you've already promulgated your plan and we're going to use the same method and tools for communicating changes.

Go back to the 5P. You don't need to redo the entire plan; you just need to communicate the changes. This can be called a "FRAG-O" or Fragmentary Order. It's just the pieces that have changed. If the Situation and Mission remain the same, there's no need to re-issue them. Keep the format of the 5P intact. Doing so will allow your organization to easily integrate the changes into the overall plan and communicate those changes to their people in the same manner.

Continue the cycle: Execute, Evaluate, Adjust, Communicate – Execute, Evaluate, Adjust, Communicate. One of three things will eventually occur and break the cycle.

1. Mission Accomplishment
2. Mission Failure/Abandonment
3. Mission Morph

The first two are self-explanatory. When you accomplish the mission, you'll move on to the next. If the mission fails or is abandoned to funnel resources to a more successful operation, you move on to the next.

You may also experience Mission Morph. This is when your endeavor is extended over long periods of time. As you cycle through Execution, Evaluation, Adjustment, and Communication, there may be minor changes in the plan- including the overall mission. The more cycles you go through, the more you will learn about the mission, the organization, and the marketplace, i.e. the Battlespace.

As you learn, you may discover you need a major adjustment in your mission, but a majority of the framework of your plan is still relevant and effective. This is Mission Morph. You now have an entirely new mission, but you are able to continue executing your plan, for the most part. There are occasions where a plan will survive multiple morphs and that's okay. If the time comes for you to scrap the plan you are working with and create an entirely new one that's more inline with the new mission, you'll discover that in the Evaluation phase. Don't hesitate to do that. The more Mission Morphs and major adjustment a plan takes on the hazier it becomes. If the fog rolls in, it's time to issue a new "clean" plan.

Lessons Learned

Part of growth is learning. Gaining new knowledge and being able to apply it accomplish learning. The key word there is gaining, note that it's not recording. In order to improve, you must have a method for capturing lessons and also for learning them. It's not "Lesson's Captured" it's Lessons Learned.

Throughout your leadership process, have a method for capturing the key points of experience. What worked, what didn't work? What changes were effective and not effective? What assumptions were accurate and not? What were the internal, competitor, and market reactions to your actions? Were they positive or negative? What did you discover that you wished you had known from the outset? Is there a way to gain that next time? What mistakes were made and why? What could have been done differently? The list goes on, but you get the point- capture these answers.

Now, don't stow that information in a file and let it gather dust. Analyze it, find the lessons, and disseminate that to your organization. Some organizations may even choose to have a "class" about the lessons and facilitate employees formally learning the lessons so they are better able to apply them in the future. This creates a higher level of collective experience throughout the organization.

Keep a library of these lessons too. As employees take on new challenges and missions, give them access to the Lessons Learned Library so they can see what their predecessors experienced. That will allow them to avoid some of the landmines and maximize on some opportunities they may not have otherwise seen.

Chapter 6

The Management/Leadership Quadrant

As you employ the Maneuver Management system, specifically the 5P and Leadership Success Model, for increasingly complex issues and plans, you'll find a need to better analyze your human resources for application within your plan. When you know the skillsets and abilities of the people in your organization, this becomes easier. It's also easier with a smaller organization than it is with a larger one, necessarily.

To help you better assess the people in your organization, we have created a simple tool that will assist you with placing your human resources in more appropriate roles: The Management/Leadership Quadrant.

Great People Can Accomplish Great Things

What do companies like Apple, Google, FaceBook, Microsoft and Dell all have in common? The obvious business similarities are steady growth (in some cases very quickly) to massive scale, tremendous financial power, and a history of cutting edge innovation. These are solid, successful companies that have all redefined—and in some cases actually invented— their respective industries.

This list is even more impressive when you consider that these weren't ongoing, fragmented concerns that coalesced into bigger companies. These huge enterprises began in dorm rooms and garages.

The key question here however is how did they achieve this? What enabled these wildly successful corporations to change entire industries— or to create entirely new ones—and then dominate them?

To put this into perspective, it's important to understand what's in play here. Apple helped to define the personal computing platform, and to this day continues its history of creating entirely new high tech product categories with devices like the iPod and now the iPad.

Google made the Internet usable. Facebook connected Internet users. Microsoft created a standardized platform for desktop computing when no such thing existed. And Dell pioneered the just-in-time manufacture of mail order computers.

What is the common element that all of these companies share?

Each one had an innovative, dynamic, visionary leader to take it from concept to completion. These leaders took a singular idea, shaped it, nurtured it, made it into a vision and then gave it form.

Today, these visionary leaders— the late Steve Jobs, Larry Page, Mark Zuckerberg, Bill Gates and Michael Dell—are all billionaires and some of the most successful businessmen on the planet. In the process, their collective accomplishments have revolutionized not just their respective industries, but the entire world and the society we live in.

It would, of course, be unrealistic to assume that everyone on the planet could lead a company to success the way these men have. They all have a highly unique set of innate leadership abilities and were able to focus those abilities into the results we have just discussed. But the one thing that they were all able to do consistently well was to create a clear, concise and succinct vision of their thoughts and ideas and then motivate legions of others to turn those visions into reality.

I believe that the ability to envision and motivate is at the core of effective leadership. There are many other skills that are necessary, but these two abilities are critical.

The concept of leadership is entirely about people. Basic leadership can be defined as the process of motivating people to achieve a common goal. Clearly, in order to accomplish anything as a group, people need leaders. Companies aren't led—their people are.

Success in business, however, requires more than that. A business also requires a manager. Managers optimize the use of resources and ensure that processes are properly executed. Management can be defined—at least the management of a business—as the process of driving profits by optimizing resources and executing according to systems. In order to be profitable, businesses need managers.

This is a critical distinction. In fact, when analyzing and solving business problems, it is arguably the most important thing that a business—or the executives that run it—need to understand. Businesses need managers, but people need leaders.

Where Do You Fit In?

Are you destined for greatness? Perhaps. Is your business on the fast track to world domination? Maybe. Do you—or does your business—have the combination of skills necessary to succeed at the highest level? In other words, are you a manager, a leader, or a combination both? And is your business managed? Or led?

I believe that the answers to these questions form the basis for business improvement in many different ways, at many different levels. For any business organization seeking to expand and grow, this is a logical place to start.

Before improvement can take place, it is first necessary to identify the strengths and weaknesses. Only after that's been done can an organization formulate a plan for remediation and allocation of resources. The Management/Leadership Quadrant does precisely that.

The Management/Leadership Quadrant is a tool for evaluating an individual or organization with regards to leadership abilities and management skills. Before we continue, we should define the difference between abilities and skills.

I believe that abilities are naturally occurring and can be developed to even better form. If you want to aspire to greatness in a particular field, you need to start with the raw material that is necessary for that endeavor. For example, not everybody that wants to pitch in the big leagues has a strong enough arm or the unique body mechanics to do it at the professional level. Ditto if you want to be a linebacker in the NFL but weigh 180 pounds and run the 40-yard dash in 30 seconds- it's just not going to happen. And if you want to be a best selling novelist but have a difficult time putting a decent sentence together, the chances of a major publisher picking up your work are slim.
The point is not to crush dreams, rather it's to say that not everyone has what it takes to do certain things and that includes being a leader.

If you have a difficult time formulating a vision for yourself to follow, it's going to be extremely difficult to do it for others. And if you struggle to ratchet up the motivation to face small challenges when they occur, motivating others to overcome large obstacles will be next to impossible.

Another consideration when determining someone's leadership ability is the present state of the trait. Some people are inherently good leaders but have never been in a leadership role, or have never had any leadership training whatsoever. This lack of experience doesn't preclude them from assuming a leadership role; it simply means that they will require more development effort and time.

As an aside, most highly effective leaders manifest these abilities early on, often at an early age. Perhaps they assume a leadership role in school or on an athletic team. Maybe it's in a social group, club or organization. We have found that most prospective leaders already have some form of leadership in their history.

Management on the other hand, still requires ability, but it requires the ability to learn skills and not necessarily to lead. Effective management is a set of skills that can be taught, learned and mastered. Where you often hear of a dynamic person referred to as a "born leader," you almost never hear of a "born manager."

It's also important to understand that a natural leader may not in fact be a good manager. Again, management requires very specific skills that, in many cases, have nothing at all to do with leadership. Generally speaking and depending on the level at which a manager works, there are typically some fairly technical concepts that must be mastered. For example, a senior executive who can create a vision and motivate people but who can't understand the operating statements of the business cannot function as an effective manager. They probably shouldn't be a senior executive if they can't do that, but the point is the same.

This is where the Management/Leadership Quadrant comes into play. We use it to:

- Assess ourselves for what roles we should be filling or seeking to fill and to identify personal development requirements;
- Categorize members of the organization in order to asses their performance, evaluate their roles, and identify the need for additional training and development;
- Match organizational roles with properly skilled and able individuals;
- Assess overall organizational leadership and management "health" and discover gaps that can be filled with management and leadership tools.

By placing ourselves into the quadrant, we can give ourselves an honest evaluation of our own skills and abilities with regards to management and leadership. We can also evaluate what type of roles and positions we should be filling and seeking by seeing what roles we can best fill. If we desire a certain position or role, we can place that in the quadrant as well and see how we relate to it. If, in order to succeed, we need to become a stronger leader, we can then seek out leadership development. The same holds true for becoming a stronger manager.

Strong Leader Weak Manager	Strong Leader Strong Manager
Weak Leader Weak Manager	Weak Leader Strong Manager

As leaders, assessing an individual's placement in the Management/Leadership Quadrant allows us to quickly categorize their performance as it relates to their position. Every organization has a need for managers and leaders. That holds true if you are the only person in your organization or if there are tens of thousands of people. Lets remember: things are managed, but people are led.

A small business owner has a need to be a leader in his or her own right- to be visionary, pro-active, and disciplined. They also have a need to manage their business operations. Larger organizations have job functions that require a great amount of leadership and others that are rote management. There are even going to be positions that don't require the employee to be a leader or a manager.

When we assess an individual against their position, we evaluate what type of person the position requires. Does the position require a strong leader, a strong manager, or both? We then place the individual in the appropriate quadrant. If the individual and position are in the same quadrant, we have a match. If they are not, then we need to evaluate whether we need to replace that individual, alter the position roles and responsibilities, or develop the individual as a better leader or manager. If the person is placed outside the same quadrant as the position, are they more qualified than the position requires? If so, is there an opportunity to better employ them in accordance with their skills and abilities?

We can use this same concept when filling positions internally. If the entire organization employs the Management/Leadership Quadrant, when we evaluate individuals to fill a position we can use their past and current senior personnel's placement of them in the quadrant to match against the quadrant placement of the position to be filled. For instance, if we need to fill the position of "Project A Manager" we first place that position in the quadrant. Lets say we find it requires a strong manager, but not necessarily a strong leader. We would place it in the Strong Manager/Weak Leader quadrant.

That becomes our minimum placement for prospects to fill the position. If we have individuals who are strong leaders/weak managers or weak leaders/weak managers, they are eliminated from consideration. Certainly, though, if we have a strong manager/strong leader, they would still be a candidate if there is no better placement for them within the organzation.

Strong Leader Weak Manager John Riley	Strong Leader Strong Manager Mary Lunts
Weak Leader Weak Manager Bill Hurts Rick Belt	Weak Leader Strong Manager Position: Project A Manager George Ray Jane Smith

The Management / Leadership Quadrant can also be used to evaluate organizational health. First, we can compare all of our positions with the individuals filling those roles. We can do this for every position and individual or we can do it on an organizational basis. We've already discussed how to do it individually. To do this on an organizational basis, we place all of our positions into quadrants and take the sum of the positions. We then do the same for individuals. This would give us a result similar to:

Strong Leader Weak Manager Positions: 12 Individuals: 10	Strong Leader Strong Manager Positions: 4 Individuals: 2
Weak Leader Weak Manager Positions: 19 Individuals: 23	Weak Leader Strong Manager Positions: 32 Individuals: 28

This doesn't tell us if the right people are in the right positions, it just tells us if we have the human resources to fill the leadership and management roles of the organization as they are currently structured. In order to determine if the right people are in the right positions, we must individually evaluate them against their positions.

If there is a shortfall of qualified managers and leaders, the organization must then evaluate what type of remediation can be applied. Most likely, leadership and management development programs will have to be initiated. In more severe cases, the organization will have to consider restructuring their roles, responsibilities, and human resources to better fit with the mission requirements.

When we at The Warriors Group use this tool, we understand that when shortfalls or mismatched positions and resources are identified, immediate actions are required. Implementing leadership and management training can take some time. In order to create immediate results, we apply the same tools that are in this book to instantly increase performance, communication, and effectiveness.

Chapter 7

The Business Cycle Pendulum and Continuum

Everything is Cyclical

It doesn't matter if you are considering weather, relationships, the economy, or business. There's no avoiding the cycles of life and business. There are, however, ways to at least partially control these cycles.

In the military, probably the most blatant example of cyclical events, at least administratively, is the turnover of personnel. On average, every individual changes station and/or assignment every 3 years. This creates constant change in troop and staff levels. If not properly managed, a unit can find themselves in a continual battle between shortage and abundance. Operating in such a manner is not conducive to unit cohesion, efficiency, or effectiveness. For a military unit, it is devastating to combat readiness. Perhaps you can relate with human resource turnover at your organization. If you can, you have witnessed first hand how difficult continuity of operations can be without effective resource management.

In order to manage the personnel levels at units, the military uses manpower departments that must take many factors into account. They must have visibility of standard rotations, off-cycle rotations, combat injuries, medical conditions that require special care at a specific location, non-medical issues that preclude an individual from rotating (legal for example), specific unit activity and mission tasking, new recruit pipelines, training school pipelines, personnel separating from service, and personnel retiring- just to name a few.
They have to take all of those factors into account and effectively manage the timing and volume of transfers and assignments. As you can see, a lot of energy, effort, information and time go into ensuring every unit has the personnel they need to accomplish their mission. When you think about it, it's an absolutely monumental task and the military does it very well.

The whole goal of the process is not to keep a steady state of human resources at every unit. Our military is a voluntary force and although we may come close, there just aren't a constant number of new recruits. The activity level and mission of our forces also changes and requires adjustments to where resources are applied. For example, in a time of war, more emphasis is placed on manning combat units than administrative units.

The goal of the process is to minimize the swing and extremity of shortages and abundance. In doing so, units are able to function within a zone that may not be the absolute ideal, but permits them to maintain readiness, effectiveness, and the ability to accomplish their mission.

The concept of operating within a controlled zone can be applied to myriad situations. Further, it can significantly improve business operations by providing a level of stability that may not currently exist. It can also prevent future periods of instability, even if they are not currently being felt.

We have defined this concept and call it the "Business Cycle Pendulum" and we plot it on the "Business Cycle Continuum." Although those terms may sound technical and daunting, rest assured the concept is not. In fact, this is a very simple concept that can yield immediate results for you and your organization.

Business Cycle Continuum

In order to understand the Business Cycle Pendulum, we must first explain the Business Cycle Continuum. We'll focus on the business cycle, but rest assured this same concept can be applied to other aspects of your life in which you have input and even those that you don't. What I mean by that is you can't control weather cycles because you don't have an input, but you can plan for events created by weather cycles in an effort to stabilize the situation. You do have input into your relationships, finances, etc. and therefore do have a degree of control and can directly influence them.

Business cycles can be controlled, at least partially. We will never be able to have a steady state of business and we don't want that. Consumer sentiment and sophistication, technology, delivery methods, and innovation will forever change and evolve and therefore create a constant need for businesses to adapt. So, too, is the way of life- conditions are always changing. If we had an absolute steady state of business, we would not be adapting as necessary and that steady state would become a steady decline.

Before we get into the details of this concept, we need to discuss the use of the term "business cycle." Certain aspects of our business are indeed true cycles. There is a loop that is created as a function of processes- those may be internal processes, economic processes, or even consumer purchase processes. There are also aspects of our business that are cyclical in the respect that they "cycle" from one side of a continuum to the other. It's those aspects that we apply this concept to.

Our goal in controlling our business cycles is not to create a steady state; rather it's to create left and right boundaries in which we can effectively operate outside of a crisis state. Make no mistake; there are crisis states on either side of the continuum. For the purposes of this article, lets use the level of sales for a business to illustrate this concept.

On the left side of the sales continuum, we have low sales volume and on the right we have high sales volume. You might say, "Okay, I see how low sales volume could create crisis, but high sales volume?" Yes, high sales volume can create crisis too and we'll discuss that in a moment.

The Business Cycle Pendulum

The business cycle with regards to issues that can be plotted on a continuum can be illustrated with a pendulum.

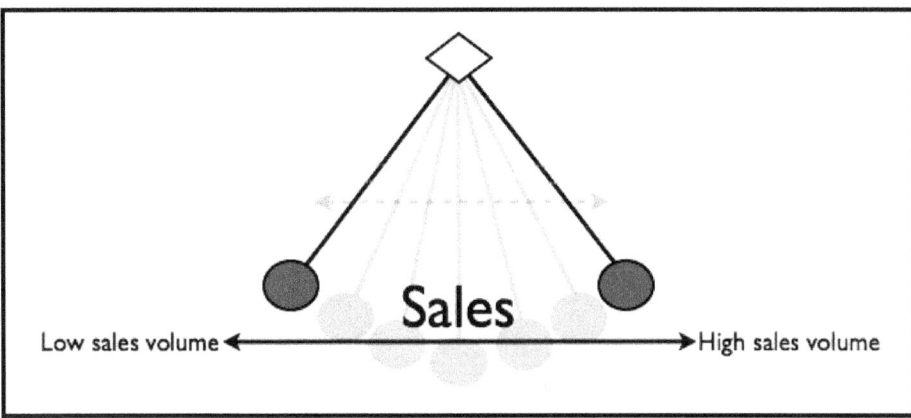

Staying with our sales volume example, as the pendulum swings to the left, organizations typically take action to increase sales, thus swinging the pendulum back to the right- the bigger the swing to the right the bigger the potential swing to the left. If an organization fails to take action to increase sales, the pendulum can most certainly unhinge and swing perpetually to the left until the organization is no longer a going concern. We'll discuss that later when we explain Crisis Spread Points.

It doesn't matter what the consideration is; the pendulum swings. We have good weather and bad, high turnover and low, few equipment failures and many. Where the good and bad plot on your organizations continuum depend on what conditions are positive and negative relative to your organizational mission and function. For example, a company that repairs manufacturing equipment might plot a high breakdown rate on the right, where that company's customers might plot it on the left. The breakdowns are a positive for the repair company- so long as they didn't fail to repair it correctly the fist time- since that's business volume for them. Conversely, the breakdowns are a negative for the manufacturing customer who relies on the machines to create products and therefore create revenue.

Crisis Points

Crisis Points can be defined as situations where, if immediate and proper action is not taken, the organization will be damaged. That damage will most typically, or ultimately, be financial, but can also take the form of public relations, employee relations, investor relations (stock price), etc. The potential damage is a function of what elements of business the cycle directly and indirectly impacts.

When we add our Crisis Points to the illustration, we see a meaningful picture begin to develop:

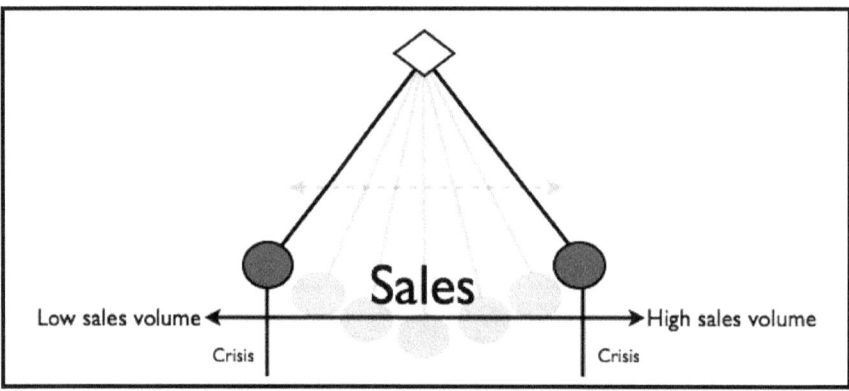

In this business cycle example, the sales business cycle, low sales volume can be the lynchpin for an organization. Crisis is created first in the sales department, where resources being expended are not justified by the revenue being generated. If sales are not increased, crisis spreads to other departments and eventually the organization as a whole. After all, if there are no products or services being sold, there are no clients to service, and ultimately no need for the sales based business organization.

Crisis can be created in the business cycle through high sales volume as well, particularly if the swing to the right is rapid or unexpected. An organization that is overwhelmed with sales is in crisis because of the lack of resources and processes to satisfy demand. If the organization meets the demand through adding resources, if the swing to the right is short lived, the organization will find itself with an abundance of resources that are not warranted.

Not only is this a drain on the bottom-line, which can create crisis, it can actually shift the left boundary of low sales volume. For example, an organization's break-even point is $1mm a month in consummated sales. That's based on the current level of resources, i.e. human, material, facility, etc. In an unexpected swing to the right, the organization tries to adapt by hiring a large amount of new employees, contracting new facilities, and securing materials for production. Now, the organizations break even is $2mm a month in consummated sales in order to cover their additional expenses. They have shifted their left crisis boundary and redefined the parameters of their business cycle. Now, if this organization approaches their previous crisis threshold of $1mm/month in sales, they would be at 50% of required sales revenue to break-even.

As mentioned above, crisis, once reached, has the ability to spread like a disease. The greater the crisis in one cycle, the more it impacts other cycles, departments, and eventually all aspects of business operations. We call these Crisis Spread Points. It's important to understand this and the role one cycle's levels of crisis plays in the rest of business operations. A leader who has a picture of where the next crisis will arise, as a result of another, has the knowledge to act with foresight- the power of that cannot be understated.

We can add Crisis Spread Points and further develop the picture:

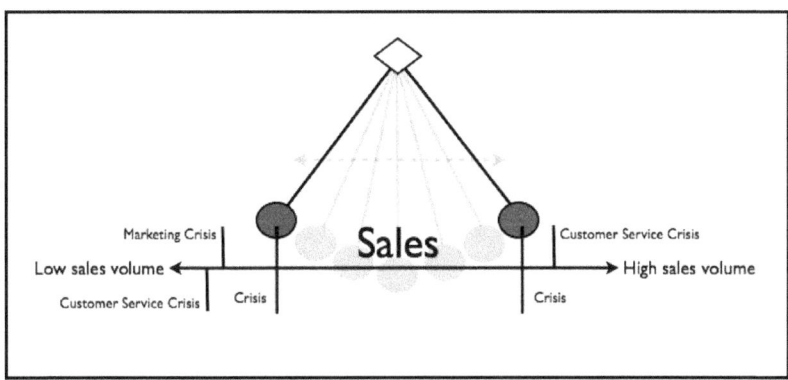

Note here that Crisis Spread Points are asymmetrical. Where a deep swing to the left for sales might create a crisis for the marketing department and then customer service, a deep swing to the right would more quickly create crisis for customer service by way of need for personnel and equipment to handle new servicing volume.

The Operating Zone

The business cycle Operating Zone is the zone in which your business operates efficiently, profitably, and with stability; it should not be arbitrarily created. It should be a result of analyzing the capabilities of the organization and demands of the market. The left and right zone limits should be set inside the crisis lines on the business cycle continuum at points where the organization will have sufficient time to act accordingly. They are essentially warning lines; they are the outer boundaries of your defense perimeter. If the pendulum approaches them, warn the troops. If it touches, man the trenches. If it crosses them, give the order to fire so your position isn't over run.

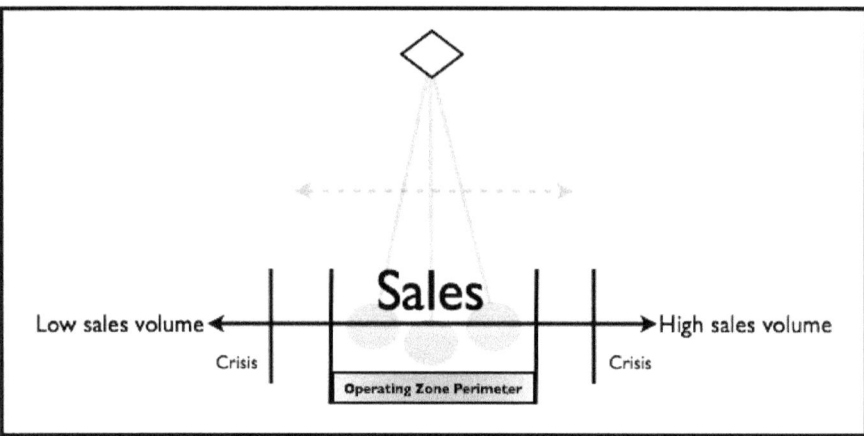

There will be times you cross your zone perimeters and your crisis perimeters. An example would be a new client who places a massive order. Another example would be a regulatory change that renders one of your products useless. It's going to happen and that's when your leadership will be key. Adapt quickly, but wisely. Don't over-hire or over-contract resources. Don't react without considering the consequences of the pendulum swinging back the other way. Developing Courses of Action (COA) ahead of time will allow you to take planned actions instead of shooting from the cuff.

Using the example of sales, if we were to stay within this zone in its current position on the business cycle continuum, our profits would never increase. In order to grow the business, we need to shift the Operating Zone to the right. It's critical to shift the zone at the appropriate time. Too soon and the pendulum will penetrate your left perimeter. Too late and you'll find yourself in crisis from a right perimeter penetration. Shift the Operating Zone when the business supports the shift, no sooner and no later. The best indicator for timing a zone shift is when your crisis boundaries shift, though a leader who can see that coming in advance will be the better on the battlefield.

Develop COA

As leaders, we must develop several layers of COA. We have developed and plotted our Operating Zone, Crisis Points, and Crisis Spread Points. We now have more knowledge about our business operations and cycles and how they affect other cycles and business functions. What do we do when we approach the limits of our Operating Zone? What happens when we breach the Operating Zone limits? Approach Crisis Points? Breach them? How about Crisis Spread Points? These are all layers of COA.

We need to develop actions for each of those scenarios. When we approach our Operating Zone limits, we need to have action steps that will mitigate the risk of breaching them. That may be, initially, seeking out the cause of the swing and recognizing whether or not it has the potential to swing far enough to breach the zone limits. It might be taking specific action steps to ensure the zone limits are not breached. What that looks like is dependent on the issue being addressed.

If the Operating Zone limits are breached, we need action steps to return operations to the zone. That may be adapting manufacturing volume, adding seasonal workers, etc. In all cases though, it will require some sort of adaptation. Planned COA are critical here and going forward to crisis states. Although every situation will be different, having a baseline of planned actions will greatly reduce the propensity for over-reacting. There is great value in the process here. When developing COA, we must consider abstract events- abstract in so far as we are not currently experiencing them.

In doing this, we expose ourselves to the thought processes involved with dealing with those events and therefore gain a certain level of experience. When we are faced with the actual events, we have already thought about them and how we would react; we are not blindsided and caught off guard. We have a baseline for action even if the actual event differs in detail from that which we planned for.

The same holds true for approaching and breaching Crisis Points and Crisis Spread Points with the additional consideration of other stakeholders. As we approach and breach these points, we will inevitably impact other aspects of the business.

Recall the modes of planning. Creating the COA for breaching Crisis Points is considered Contingency planning.

Input Controls

If the organization has input into the cycle being considered, we must implement controls to mitigate the risk of breaching our Operating Zone limits. If we do not have input, we can only develop COA to minimize the impact or exploit opportunity.

Our current example of sales volume certainly allows for input from the organization. The size of the sales force, product selection, price points, etc. are all things that are controlled by the organization. With an established Operating Zone and the knowledge that the organization has input, we can develop controls to increase the propensity for remaining within the Operating Zone.

For illustrative purposes, and keeping with our current sales volume example, lets use a basic scenario. This organization has historically breached their Crisis Points and Crisis Spread Points at least 4 times a year at various periods. By analyzing their annual sales volume, it's clear that they have the capacity to support the volume on an annual basis- in fact, by annualizing sales volume and averaging it on a monthly basis, we find they could remain in their Operating Zone every month. The issue is that customers tend to place orders in bulk and those orders are unpredictable in time and quantity. A deeper look at each customers orders reveals that they order a relatively steady quantity on an annual basis.

A control that can be implemented is to work with customers to change their orders. Instead of bulk orders a few times a year, this organization would benefit from its customers spreading their purchases throughout the year. An even greater control would be creating an organizational schedule that lays out the orders for the year and schedules them more effectively. New customers would be integrated into the schedule to maintain stability.

This might sound counter-intuitive to customer service. After all, we want to give our customers what they want, when they want it. It's not at all. Why do this organizations customers order the way they do? Is it because of bulk pricing? Is it because of an internal process that makes it beneficial to the customer? If it is, perhaps changing that policy or process is what needs to happen. Is it because this organization's customers have just always done it that way or don't know there are alternatives? Perhaps formulating a plan that works better for them, and this organization, is best.

General Electric takes this concept to a very high level. They provide Six Sigma Black Belt representatives to their client organizations in order to more effectively match the processes and efficiencies of the customers and GE. By doing this, they improve their customers business operations, thus creating loyalty and longevity in their customer base. At the same time, they are integrating their customers into GE's processes and methodologies. It's a win-win situation and is very effective.

Metrics and Communication

With all other aspects in place, we must create metrics to understand where we are on the Business Cycle Continuum and we must be able to communicate those metrics to others. What we measure will obviously dictate what we track. For our current example, this is very straightforward. Our metrics will be based on sales volume. At a minimum, we will need to know what our current month's volume is and what our pipeline is. This will give us a current view of where we are on the continuum as well as where we are likely to be in future months, at this current point in time.

For other cycles, the metrics involved will be much more complex. Perhaps you need to track efficiency on an assembly line or quality of raw materials. Whatever you need to track, you need to employ or create metrics to do so.

Its important to have a method of communicating the situation to other organizational leaders so they can prepare for the corresponding swing on the their continuums. Of course, you have that now in the 5 Paragraph Plan.

Not only is communicating this critical, the timing of that communication is critical as well. Whatever processes and methods are in place for communicating, they must occur with ample time for the other organizational leaders to act accordingly. Information that arrives too late is no better than bad information- neither allows us to act in a timely and proper manner.

Which brings us to the next point- bad information. Information that is simply incorrect is, obviously, bad information. Information that cannot be interpreted usefully is also bad information. It's not that the data is bad; it's the method of conveyance. If I were given a report on the efficiency of one of Ford's manufacturing lines, that was written by an engineer for an engineer, using equipment names and proprietary statistical analysis, I would be utterly lost. I would not be able to do a single thing with that document other than wedge it under a lopsided table to stop it from wobbling. If I were an employee of Ford responsible for delivering products to customers and the efficiency of that line affected my ability to do so, wouldn't it be important for me to understand it? It would, and that's why it's important to ensure that information conveyed is done so in a manner and form that is useful to those who receive it. Just as a plan should be written for those who receive it, not those who write it, so it is with any information.

Leadership Goals

Implementing this concept requires leadership. Organizational leaders must be able to evaluate the business and identify the issues. They then must be able to be critical of the situation and create action plans in conjunction with organizational management. In that, the leadership process for this concept is:

1- Identify the cycles. Without that knowledge we can't go any further.
2- Identify and plot your left and right Crisis Points for each cycle.
3- Identify and plot Crisis Spread Points. This will require cross-functional coordination.
4- Identify and plot your Operating Zone. Remember, this is the zone on the continuum where the organization is effective and free of crisis with regards to the cycle being considered. There should be substantial distance between your Operating Zone boundaries and your crisis boundaries in order to allow for action if the Operating Zone is breached, but before crisis is reached.
5- Develop Courses of Action (COA) in the event the Operating Zone and Crisis Point limits are approached or breached.
6- Decide if the organization has an input and therefore some level of control.
   a. If the organization has an input, create controls for remaining within the Operating Zone.
   b. If the organization does not have an input, COA plans will dictate successfully navigating the issues.

7- Develop metrics for tracking the organizations position on the continuum and a process for communicating (or validate existing communication methods) that information as well as any COA that are being triggered.

This leadership process will have to become a loop for your organization. As conditions change within the organization and the operating environment, new cycles will emerge and old ones will change. The results are not static.

Foresight and Planned Action

We all know we cannot see into the future. We do not know exactly what will transpire or how our actions will interact with the events that will occur. We do, however, know that events will occur and that they will impact our business and our business cycles. By understanding our cycles and how they affect our specific business functions as well as the organization as a whole, we can plan our actions and be more prepared to lead our employees, departments, and organizations.

This is not a 5-minute exercise; it will take time to fully realize and analyze all of the cycles that affect your operations. Start with the most obvious- you will gain understanding and experience through the process. The first will lead to many others that you may not even be considering right now. With greater understanding of your operating environment, conditions, and inputs, you will have the knowledge to act with more foresight using planned COA as your baseline. You will have a greater ability to lead your organization.

LEVEL III

Chapter 8

Maneuver Management Operating Principles

It might seem strange that we are just now delving into the overarching operating principles of Maneuver Management. There's good reason for that. The principles I am about to lay out for you are very closely tied, and sometimes identical, to principles by which military forces engage in warfare. I have found, over the years, that people who are exposed to these principles before the basic planning elements of the Battlespace and 5P have a higher propensity to reject the system outright. I can understand that because the comparison between war and business can be uncomfortable for a lot of people.

By teaching the basic tools first, students of Maneuver Warfare have the opportunity to apply them to their business and discover the validity of the system. It's then that they are more open to learning these higher-level principles for operation. It also allows me to more freely use terms like "competitors" and "enemies" interchangeably because the reader has more of an understanding that I do so as a matter of habit in an effort to keep the connection between the original principles of Maneuver Warfare and the Maneuver Management principles as adapted for business.

Learning the basic tools first does not preclude success. Rather, now learning the Maneuver Management operating principles will enhance your use of the basic tools and increase your ability to succeed. It is quite possible for you to not read the following chapters and still gain a great advantage in your business by employing what you have already learned. I expect that a portion of readers will do just that and hopefully return to these higher level concepts when they need or want to.

At this level of planning, Level III, the principles I am going to teach you will not only improve your Level I and II planning and execution, but they will expand your strategic thinking and you'll be able to apply these principles to your business to gain greater success.

Before I get too far into this chapter, I need to make one thing abundantly clear. War is war and business is business. Nothing else in the course of human events can ever come close to the sheer intensity of armed combat and the tremendous risks that our men and women in uniform face when they are in a combat zone. To imply otherwise is nonsense.

With that said, business today is highly competitive and becoming even more so. Although it's clearly not a matter of life or death, businesses fight for financial survival and operational continuity every day, and this continuous struggle can take a tremendous toll on the people who operate these companies, especially if training and resources are deficient or misaligned.

Although war is probably the oldest, and most extreme, form of competition between people, commerce ranks close behind. And whenever there are multiple sellers competing for a finite number of customers, that competition may become fierce. Any organization that intends to succeed in the pursuit of its goals needs to understand and address this business reality.

Anyone who's ever operated a business that is fighting for survival or an increased market share would likely agree that it is in fact an intense undertaking, even if it doesn't come close to the rigors of armed combat.

This is where the parallel between war and business comes into play. Businesses facing the challenges of success, and even survival, must overcome many of the same challenges that a military force must overcome, with the exception of course that no one is shooting at them.

Just as Marine officers rely on their training and proven systems to guide them as they lead Marines in combat, so too must today's successful business leaders rely on proven systems and leadership guided by sound operating principles.

Success in business is often achieved by identifying a miniscule advantage over the competition and exploiting it as much as possible. The way to do this is by having a strong, well-defined management system in place coupled with the skills and training necessary to use it effectively.

It's the operating principles of Maneuver Management, along with the tools in the system, that will allow you to gain success through systematic and well-planned action.

Maneuver Warfare

Maneuver Warfare is a warfighting doctrine that seeks to eliminate an enemy's ability to fight by disrupting its decision-making and command functions with characteristically rapid movement of combat elements coupled with the effects of intense and violent attacks using a wide range of weapons.

On the other end of the warfighting strategy continuum is the concept of attrition warfare. As the name implies, a fighting force pursuing a strategy of attrition sets about to wear down the enemy to the point of surrender by inflicting massive and ongoing losses of troops and materiel. Additionally, in attempting to grind down an opponents ability to fight, an attrition strategy requires sufficient time to work.

Most military strategists and theorists, going all the way back to Sun Tzu, advocate avoiding an attrition strategy. Sun Tzu suggested that the objective of any human conflict, particularly combat, is to, "win without fighting, avoiding attrition, and to use resources wisely and economically." He also points out that attrition warfare is exceptionally expensive, in terms of both money and human capital.

The concepts of maneuver are important for business leaders to understand, unless you happen to run a company like Microsoft or Google. Most smaller companies simply don't have the resources to compete with larger businesses on an attrition basis and they shouldn't even if they did.

Instead, they need to rely upon good planning using sound operating principles with flawless execution and strong cohesion to compete and win market share. In a nutshell, that is what Maneuver Management is at this level: Business Maneuver Warfare.

Surface vs. Gap

In Maneuver Management, as in Maneuver Warfare, strengths and weaknesses are called surfaces and gaps, respectively. A Marine combat officer needs to understand the difference between a surface and a gap. As a civilian business manager or executive, so do you. You want to attack the enemy where he is weakest with the bulk of your forces. Your goal is to bypass enemy surfaces and attack and exploit gaps.

If a surface is a strength and a gap is a weakness, why not just call them strengths and weaknesses? I am a big proponent of the K.I.S.S. principle (Keep It Simple Stupid), so I assure you there is a reason behind it. In Maneuver Management, we seek to create a common operating picture for all operators. This goes beyond making sure everyone is "on the same page." It is, in fact a literal common operating picture (aptly called a COP in the military)- a visual representation of, you guessed it, the Battlespace.

If you were to draw a line representing a river, with the intent of identifying the best place to cross, how might you represent the deeper and faster sections as opposed to the more shallow and easier to cross? You might do this by varying the thickness of the line or changing the color. Maybe you use a dotted line with bigger spaces in between the dots corresponding to more shallow water and a solid line representing the deepest sections. If you took a step back and looked at your line, it would be pretty obvious which sections presented the best opportunity to cross, based on the depth of the water. Your solid lines are the rivers surfaces and the sections where the line has large distances between dots are the rivers gaps. In this example, you are quite literally showing gaps in your line as a representation of more shallow sections.

The terms of surfaces and gaps are much easier to represent visually than strengths and weaknesses. They are also much more versatile in the sense that they can denote strengths and weaknesses across a broader spectrum of variables. Lastly, using the line example, if you were to do the same for your competitors market reach and then draw a line representing your distribution reach, you would be able to instantly see where you could apply your strongest distribution against your competitors weakest market reach.

A surface represents a hard spot, strength, or challenge. Militarily, it could be an enemy position, unit, a fortification, or a mass of troops where the enemy can deter your mission efforts.

A gap is the opposite. It's a soft spot or enemy weakness that, once identified, can be exploited. It could be a simple separation between enemy units where they can't mutually support one another, or some other physical deficiency that creates opportunity.

A gap can also be a weakness in time or space where the enemy is unprepared and therefore vulnerable. Gaps include poor morale, tactical error, lack of preparation, lack of mutual support, and predictable opening patterns.

In maneuver warfare, and Maneuver Management, the objective is to bypass enemy surfaces and instead to attack and exploit gaps. A key consideration, however, is that gaps are rarely permanent; they come and go because they are created by events in time and space.

Military leaders are taught that once a gap has been identified, it must be rapidly and ruthlessly exploited. Additionally, if there are no gaps to be found, then they must be created.

The Context of Business

Within the context of business, surface/gap relationships are important to recognize. The entire cohesive team, indeed the corporate culture, should be attuned to the process of recognizing and identifying surfaces and gaps within the company's Battlespace.

The surface/gap framework can describe market conditions, manufacturing processes, staffing and hiring decisions, and purchasing situations equally well. Of course when it comes to planning, starting the planning effort by identifying surfaces and gaps the company is facing creates a logical and efficient starting point. You will also identify many more of each as you engage in the planning process itself.

The important thing here is to understand the difference between the two. A surface can be your strengths to your competition or your competitions' strengths to you. It's where your resources will be least effectively applied against your competition in an engagement. A surface can also be applied internally in developing processes, products, or new initiatives. Often times, applying your own surfaces internally yields the greatest results.

A competitor's gap, or a gap in the marketplace, is an opportunity that enables you and your company to affect change consistent with your goals and objectives by applying your resources in an exploitative manner.

Internal gaps should not be used to bolster activities, but should rather be avoided, as the result will tend to be a less than optimal outcome. If an internal gap is identified as mission critical, resources must be applied to make it a surface and thus employable. So, external surfaces and internal gaps are to be avoided. External gaps and internal surfaces are to be exploited.

It's also useful to think of surfaces and gaps in a non-linear sense. Surfaces and gaps can and do occur fluidly, constantly changing and evolving. Imagine trying to cross a stream by jumping from ice floe to ice floe. The stream itself is the surface; the ice floes are gaps that can be exploited, in this case to cross the stream. But doing so will require a healthy dose of agility and physical prowess, as you jump from floe to floe, across the stream. You'll also need to be able to adapt quickly mid-stream, if you will.

Another example to consider is that of colonial troops. Lines of soldiers came onto the battlefield, loaded their muskets in formation, took aim and fired on command at one another. This is linear. It is strength on strength; it is attrition.

Think now of the Mexican cartels—smuggling underground, exploiting weaknesses in border security, government policy, constantly probing and identifying gaps. They avoid direct confrontation, and wind up smuggling millions of dollars, probably billions, into the U.S. Although it's illegal, and abhorrent, this is a perfect example of effective maneuver.

By the way, the concept of surfaces and gaps, of avoiding strengths and exploiting weakness is not new. Clausewitz talked about it in the early 19th century when he said that it is a risky business to attack an abler opponent in a good position. This is the very essence of identifying a surface, and avoiding it in favor of exploiting a gap.

I need to be clear on the point of using the term "exploitation." When I use that term, I am referring to taking advantage of an opportunity in your Battlespace. I am not referring to exploiting customers in the marketplace. There is a very big distinction there. When we exploit opportunity, we recognize an opportunity and apply our resources to gain the most benefit from its existence and our recognition of it. We are not taking advantage of customer's needs and wants to their detriment. There is such a thing as success with honor and respect.

Tempo

Maneuver contributes significantly to sustaining the initiative, exploiting success, preserving freedom of action, and reducing vulnerability. It is through maneuver that an inferior force can achieve decisive superiority at the necessary time and place. In many cases, maneuver is made possible only through the control of tempo and effective employment of resources.

Tempo is defined as the rate of action. Controlling or altering that rate is a necessary means to initiative; all operations alternate between action and pauses as opposing forces battle one another and fight friction to mount and execute operations at the time and place of their choosing.

The force that opposes tempo is friction. In the physical world, friction is the resistance that occurs between two substances. An example would be the resistance of a road on a rubber tire. In that case—in all cases in fact—friction tends to impede motion, while at the same time eroding resources.

It is the same in both war and business. While military commanders seek to maintain an aggressive tempo in their campaigns, friction tends to impede that tempo. The great strategist, von Clausewitz, suggested that friction in combat is caused by the inherent danger of the struggle, by the physical demands of armed combat, and by the ever-pervasive "fog of war." Friction is also created because each action we take or our opponent takes inherently changes the environment and the actions that are required to achieve success.

It's important to note that although we tend to think of tempo as a necessary measurement of speed—specifically, that tempo always has to be quick—there are occasions where we might want the tempo to be slower in order to impede our opponent in one way or another.

Generally, we will want to decrease our opponent's tempo, while increasing ours, thus creating a further divide between our abilities to influence the Battlespace (greater ability for us, lesser ability for them). The key is to maintain control of the tempo so that you control the Battlespace.

People get tired of course, but often in business and in their jobs they get bored as well. They lose motivation, often because they lose sight of their goals. From the perspective of the human element, boredom kills tempo and lack of tempo breed's boredom and frustration. Too quick a tempo erodes your resources effectiveness.

In short, it is one of your goals to control your operating tempo as well as the tempo of events in the overall Battlespace.

Effective Control

The Marine Corps exerts effective control over its combat operations through a function it calls Command and Control (C^2), defined as the exercise of authority and direction by a properly designated commander over assigned forces in the accomplishment of the mission.

The Marine Corps requires that every echelon of C^2 is flexible, fast and decentralized. In all cases, effective C^2 flows from the commander at the top who ultimately provides the impetus for it.

This is why the Marine Corps' focus on effective leadership is so critical. Since leaders are directly responsible for successfully exercising command and control—for getting things done—at every level of the organization, unless they are highly skilled in this role, the mission will likely fail.

The entire concept of the Command and Control process applies virtually verbatim to civilian business. Every initiative that a business undertakes requires a clearly defined C^2 element that spells out who is responsible for getting what done.

Recall our discussion about Leaders Intent; it is critical for effective decentralized C^2. Within the context of C^2, Leaders Intent provides a road map to achieving conditions necessary for decisive maneuver. It also allows subordinates to made decisions in a highly fluid environment in the absence of specific orders.

Many civilian businesses have developed an organizational chart that depicts their management structure and executive hierarchy. While it makes sense for everyone in the organization to know their role, who they report to, and who reports to them, the existence of an org chart does not constitute effective command and control.

Effective C^2 requires much more. One of the fundamental principles of the Maneuver Management system is to ensure that a functional and efficient command and control structure exists within in an organization, and that everyone in the business chain of command knows how it works.

Lucky for you, you already have the vehicles for your basic command and control structure in the form of the 5P. Remember, Maneuver Management is progressive. Each tool, concept, and component builds on those previously presented. You will learn more throughout this book, but the foundation will not be changed.

Unity of Effort

Unity of effort is self-explanatory, at least in terms of what it is— everyone focused on accomplishing the same mission and working together in mutually supporting roles to achieve it.

What may not be so clear is how unity of effort is achieved. In business, it's the role of the executive team and the line managers.

In the Marine Corps, unity of effort stems from unity of command—the vesting of a single commander with the requisite authority to direct and coordinate the actions of all forces employed toward a common objective.

Many businesses fail to achieve unity of effort because they operate without unity of command. This is particularly true in companies that attempt to employ "flat" organizations- having a weak or complete lack of hierarchy for management and control.

The truth is that while a "flat" organization is a nice thing to do for people who don't like to have bosses and who prefer not to be told what to do, a truly flat organization flat out doesn't work.

That said, most larger organizations could use a bit of flattening. Not for the purpose of creating a less authoritative environment, but for the purpose of fostering innovation and responsibility. The flatter an organization, the shorter the path to the top, the quicker ideas and issues get to the head. Each company has to find the sweet spot for this. That might sound daunting, but it's really not. If your organization is stagnant and lower level employees feel divested, flatten. If your organization is disorganized, fragmented, or unfocused, go vertical. Make adjustments one level at a time. Don't go from completely flat to completely vertical. That would be like root shock to a tree. Ease into and find the sweet spot for your organization.

In any organization that includes more than one person and that seeks to accomplish anything, somebody needs to be in charge.

Flexibility

Maneuver Management is based, to a large extent, on sound planning. We will continue to add to your toolbox of the techniques of proper planning in later chapters, but for now it is essential to understand that any plan must first and foremost remain flexible. A rigid plan that cannot be adapted to the changing conditions of the real world is a plan destined to fail.

The Marines have a saying: "No plan lasts beyond the line of departure." To understand this, the line of departure is the point past which you are seeking to actively engage the enemy. The statement is true because, as I've mentioned previously, each action you and the enemy take inherently affects the operating environment and the actions required to achieve definitive success.

The same thing applies to business. One can never fully predict every aspect of a business Battlespace. From kinks in the supply chain to the never-ending evolution of markets, everything is always changing.

No plan can ever precisely predict the future, and no plan can ever address every possible contingency. Using the planning methodology of Maneuver Management, a business can become very adept at creating functional and actionable plans. No plan is perfect and the executive management team must be equally adept at adapting and adjusting plans to the realities of a changing situation.

Reinforce Success

Let's face it—nobody sets out on an endeavor to fail. Nevertheless, failure is a part of the human experience, and therefore must be addressed by anyone engaged in any human undertaking.

The Marine Corps warfighting doctrine offers this advice:

... we seek to exploit success rather than reinforce failure.

That statement forms the core of the Maneuver Management philosophy. In everything a business does, in every initiative it undertakes, in every goal it pursues, the focus must always be on exploiting success instead of reinforcing failure.

Albert Einstein defined insanity as the process of doing the same thing over and over again while expecting different results. His statement perfectly illuminates the problems that result from reinforcing failure.

Although the concept might appear quite obvious, in fact almost intuitive, it's really not. Many companies, when faced with a project gone awry, continue doing the very things that caused the problem in the first place. Rather than refocusing their resources on something that works— exploiting success— they continue doing what they were doing. In other words, they continue to reinforce failure.

In a minute, we'll look at some real world examples of exploiting success instead of reinforcing failure. First, there is another key concept that needs some attention. This idea is always at the center of how Marines accomplish their mission and should be for your business as well—the concept of *main effort.*

Main Effort

In a military mission, the main effort is the commander's focus for success. Identifying and designating a main effort is also a method of promoting unity within the organization. Because of all the activities and actions going on simultaneously, those of one group or individual must always be recognized and identified as the most critical to success.

Similarly, in business, it's important to recognize the main effort of any plan or operational process. For example, if an organization's primary goal is to generate revenue (which it should be), having the sales force marketing, prospecting, coordinating, and administrating might not be the best use of time, resources, and energy. It's not the quickest path to success either.

Instead, all other departments should support the sales force (the Main Effort) in obtaining more and better leads for the sales people to engage and sell to. The whole team should work to remove administrative burdens, deliver product, and service customers to create repeat business as efficiently and effectively as possible. When this happens, everyone is in fact helping to sell.

In a business that has what is often called a "sales culture," there should be no ambiguity about what the main effort is— it's the sales force. Properly conveyed, it becomes clear to all other departments that they must support the sales force in the accomplishment of its mission. Just as individual military units must ask themselves how to best support the main effort, so too must the varied departments within a company ask how they can do the same. In other words, in this case, how can they support sales.

Because the main effort is the focal point upon which everybody's support efforts are directed, one cannot take lightly the decision as to who, exactly, the main effort is. By definition, deciding on the main effort means that you have also decided the one specific thing that everyone else is supporting.

Accordingly, if the main effort has been successfully identified, and if they in fact become the focus of the organization, supporting the main effort also means supporting mission accomplishment. Properly implemented, support of the main effort is a commitment, by everyone in the organization, to do what needs to be done to achieve success.

The reality is that focusing all efforts on a particular objective carries with it a relative degree of risk, because if the main effort should fail, a substantial amount of resources could be lost.

For that reason, just as a substantial amount of due diligence is appropriate in determining the main effort, so too must the business executive or manager carefully consider what the objectives of the main effort are.

In an attack, a military commander decides on the main effort in part by identifying the center of gravity of the opposing forces and then by identifying critical vulnerabilities that expose the center of gravity.

These two concepts, *center of gravity* and *critical vulnerability*, deserve further discussion, because they apply equally well to business.

Center of Gravity and Critical Vulnerability

Earlier, we talked about surfaces and gaps. A military commander planning a mission needs to be able to identify these surfaces and gaps in order to construct a viable and purposeful mission. Surfaces and gaps are in effect the clues that indicate where an enemies strengths and weaknesses lie.

By highlighting the surfaces and gaps of an enemy, in any form, the commander then begins to identify the particular strengths and weaknesses behind those surfaces and gaps.

Here is where the concept of the center of gravity comes into play, along with its complementary concept, the critical vulnerability. The Marine Corps defines a center of gravity as the source of an enemy strength. Conversely, a critical vulnerability would be a source or cause of weakness.

As an example, if an identified strength is that an enemy force is well supplied, a corresponding center of gravity might be the logistical system that provisions the force. In this case, instead of attacking the force directly—a dangerous approach since this would be attacking a strength—it might make more sense to attack the center of gravity that enables that strength by attacking the supply train.

The critical vulnerability concept flows the other way. In this case, an ineffective logistical system that hampers resupply to the enemy force would be considered a weakness, or a gap. The critical vulnerability would be that the force cannot replenish its supplies and would be susceptible to attack.

From a business perspective, the concepts of center of gravity and critical vulnerability have significant value as a problem solving framework, as well as a perspective for planning. If the objective is to mount an assault to capture market share from a competitor, the framework can be applied verbatim. In all other competitive situations the framework can be applied to identify competitive advantages and opportunities so that actions can be planned to capitalize on them.

An organizational assessment using these concepts can be used to bolster your own preparedness and effectiveness. If you know your own centers of gravity and critical vulnerabilities, you can employ them and guard them, respectively.

Let's use our example of the river crossing again. Lets assume you have identified the best sections for facilitating a crossing. However, none of them align with your resource locations and adjusting them would make you vulnerable. Let's further assume you need to get to the other side of the river. Let's say you are a mining company and there is a huge gold deposit on the other side of the river. Your competitor is approaching from the other side and the first to get there will win the rights to mine from the landowner. All indications are they are going to beat you unless you can get your resources across the river.

The river is now a surface benefiting your competitor; the fact that it is deep in most sections is a center of gravity. As you evaluate the situation, you discover the water is deep because there is a damn upstream that is open for routine maintenance. Closing the damn would reduce the water levels and allow you to cross unimpeded by the depth of the water. The damn is a critical vulnerability. If you are able to arrange for the damn to be closed temporarily, your resources could cross the river unimpeded by the water depth. You will have exploited the critical vulnerability to affect change in the Battlespace and achieve success.

I realize this example is far fetched, but in order to grasp these concepts it's easiest to relate them to elements that we can all create a mental picture of. Once that is accomplished, applying them to more complex, real world issues is much easier.

Exploiting Success

The entire concept of exploiting success instead of reinforcing failure is simply about understanding that by definition, a decision involves choices. Unfortunately, business managers and executives fail to recognize this basic and fundamental fact.

When confronted by scenarios that clearly require a decision, they don't fully analyze the situation. Instead of determining an outcome that is best for the business from either an operational or a financial perspective, they instead feel constrained by factors that are typically based more on emotion than pure logic and good judgment.

There are many factors to consider—which will be covered in detail as we move through planning—but the simple solution is to look clearly and objectively at the required decision and the related data points.

There are many ways for a business to exploit success instead of reinforcing failure and the management team must develop the critical ability to analyze problem scenarios within this framework. As we delve deeper into the planning process and function, some additional tools and concepts will be presented to assist the reader in accomplishing this.

A simple example would be a company that sells a number of products, only several of which are profitable. Even if the unprofitable products are closely related to the company's brand, continuing to offer them is reinforcing failure. The smart decision is to drop the underperforming products, and focus instead on exploiting the success of those products that are doing well.

Politics aside, think of the General Motors brand, and the company's recent reorganization, for a real world example. Faced with bankruptcy, the company dropped under performing or excessively expensive product lines—Hummer, Saturn, Saab and Pontiac, not to mention Mr. Goodwrench himself—and focused only on those products that were performing profitably. GM has emerged from bankruptcy far less bloated, and now sells only Chevrolet, Oldsmobile, Cadillac, and GMC.

Another example of how the entire process works is arguably my favorite brand, Apple. By the turn of the millennium, Apple had a business line that was producing software for a rapidly burgeoning market of personal digital devices.

Apple's "digital hub" as they called it, included digital cameras, camcorders and pocket organizers, all of which enjoyed major mainstream markets. As it considered ways to grow the business, Apple saw the demand for digital consumer products as an established market, already served by major players such as Sony, Cannon, JVC, and many others.   However, Apple was already producing the software for many of these products, and the company believed they had the edge on product design and engineering.

The gap that Apple identified in the marketplace was that despite the growing popularity of the MP3 digital audio format, nobody was properly meeting the demand.

The external surface was the status quo of the other manufacturers. Apple needed to maneuver around that by bringing something different to the fight- a product that essentially did the same thing, but in a different and better way; a way that met consumer demand.

The center of gravity was that the major players had created the market and were dictating the direction. If Apple could attack that by changing the market in their favor, they would win.

The critical vulnerability was that the market wasn't satisfied with the status quo. There were indications of this through the popularity of sites like Napster. The consumer was looking for ease of use and integration into their lifestyle.

The internal surface was Apple's design and engineering. They did, and continue, to do that better than their competition.

They applied their internal surface to the external gap and attacked the competitions center of gravity through their critical vulnerability while avoiding a head on confrontation with the competitor's surface.

The outcome of all of this was the iPod of course, and the rest is history.

Chapter 9

WGPP

Planning to Plan

"Nothing succeeds in war except in consequence of a well prepared plan."
-Napoleon Bonaparte

Planning is the process of envisioning a desired future and then figuring out how to make it happen. With the proper training and mindset, anyone can plan effectively. Effective planning can however be somewhat time intensive, which is why many managers and executives fail to engage in the process. Using the tools you already have from this book and the ones I am about to provide you, the time it takes you to plan will be greatly reduced and you will be able to better plan everything from meetings to new product launches.

The good news is that planning is a process than can be both learned and mastered. Maneuver Management contains both the process of planning as well as the specific procedures for accomplishing it; a process is a dynamic system of related activities; a procedure is a prescribed sequence of doing something.

The mental exercise that constitutes planning has two basic components. This is going to feel a lot like the Leadership Success Model, and it should because the general concept is quite similar. The process I am about to present you, however, is a much more formal and in depth planning process. In it, you will explore possible courses of action and the potential results each will yield. Whereas the Leadership Success Model is a framework to execute and refine your plan within, the WGPP is the high level process that will help you develop your plan.

First, the planner envisions a desired Endstate. Doing this obviously requires that the planner, in fact, understands what that desired Endstate is. You need that before anything else in the planning process. You need to know where you want to go. There is a very real chance that destination may change as you plan. You may find your resources are misaligned with your Endstate- that's okay. You need a clear Endstate to begin.

Herein exists a difference between the Leadership Success Model or simple 5P. In the full WGPP, we are engineering a starting point. I refer to this as "The Idea" in the Leadership Success Model. In the WGPP, there is an assumption that you don't have that yet or you are directing your employees to create one.

The second piece is thinking through all potential actions that your organization could take to make that Endstate become a reality. Doing this requires that we project ourselves—and our organizations—forward in time in an attempt to influence and control events before they occur. I say attempt because it is impossible to clearly and precisely envision the future, hence it is impossible to completely control what will happen then. Some more good news here- I'm about to help you with that process.

By clearly thinking—and I emphasize the operative word here, clearly— through our intentions before we implement them and within the context of the outcome we desire, we can begin to make judgments as to what course of proposed action is best.

The most important thing you will ever do in business and in life is to think. As counterintuitive and alien as it may sound, many people don't think—at least not in a rigorous, analytical, and focused way.

This makes planning virtually impossible, because thinking is the heart of planning. In fact, planning is organized thinking. Don't worry, you don't need ADHD drugs to help you get through this; the planning process is a tool that creates a structure that can be used to manage thought and information for maximum effect.

Planning sometimes requires that we also attempt to understand how the Battlespace may react in response to our actions. In some business planning environments, such as when a business is competing for market share, this will be part of the process. However, many business-planning situations will not require projecting what other individuals or organizations will do. This is because many business-planning exercises are exclusively internally facing.

The Planning Session

You may be leading a group of people to create a plan; you may be by yourself at a coffee shop. The environment you plan best in, either by yourself or with others, is highly dependent on your own likes and dislikes as well as those of your team. Personally, when I engage in the WGPP I like to be in a room where I can move around a bit. Large whiteboards are a requirement and so is a large table to spread things out on. I like a more closed environment, where distractions are kept to a minimum. If I am at my office, I will schedule planning sessions during times when we can literally lock the office doors- not to prevent escape, but to prevent distractions. If I think we'll need 2 hours, I schedule at least 3 so that no one is distracted by making their next appointment or feels crunched for time. If we finish early, great. If not, that's okay too.

If you are leading a group, it's up to you to set the climate. As a minimum, you should:

•	Lead the planning session- be the moderator. As ideas are fielded, explain, from your perspective, what is good and bad about them and why. As you do this, people will further develop your concept and Endstate in their own minds- this will focus the group and spur more initiative.

•	Make sure everyone has the same information and understanding of the situation.

•	When an idea is proposed, work through it. What will happen subsequently and will it contribute to getting you to your goal?

•	Let people talk. There will be lots of mediocre ideas surrounding the gems. Don't dismiss them. Allow people to stretch their minds and take ownership of their ideas.

Sounds easy right? It is, at least in principle. Again, good news- you'll shortly have the tools to do that. Bad news? Okay, it will take you some time and experience to do it really well.

If you are a small business owner, this probably seems way too high level. You might not even have people to participate in your planning session. That's okay; it still works with just you. The same rules apply, with a little modification. Let your mind stretch and don't dismiss any of your own ideas before you evaluate them. Seek trusted advisors and friends- other business owners too. Help each other plan and you'll both benefit.

Short Term Solutions—Long Term Effect

A mistake that many planners make is that they often fail to look beyond their immediate objective when developing a course of action. The object in planning is not merely to solve the problem in the near term, but to do so in a way that lays the foundation for long-term success.

This philosophy applies to detailed, tightly defined tactical issues equally as well as to long term, complex strategic concerns. The reality is that not all problems require a detailed plan, in fact many don't. They simply require a solution. It's also true that many critical or urgent and immediate problems crop up that simply don't allow for a fully formed planning cycle. Here's where training, experience and initiative rule the day, enabling the individual faced with such situations to react and respond to fix whatever is wrong.

In those circumstances where planning is a realistic alternative, it should always be carried out. Even if it is in an abbreviated form. At a minimum, you should at least consider several courses of action and their consequences, including how you will be setting yourself up for your next move, before acting. In a lot of ways, it's like a game of chess. The further down the path of play you can envision, the better your actions will be.

Adapt and Adjust

Many individuals seem to resist planning in general because they feel that it hampers their personal flexibility. By setting forth a specific and detailed set of actions to be pursued in the future, they reason, their personal choices in the here and now are limited.

In fact, the opposite is really true, at least when considering a well-developed, thoughtful plan. Planning should be viewed as the process not only of directing an organization, but also as the process of adapting an organization to its surroundings. Essentially, there are two basic ways of doing this.

The first is to accurately—as accurately as possible anyway— anticipate future actions and reactions and then to prepare for them prior to execution. Of course no one is clairvoyant, and anticipating anything about the future is a guessing game at best. A good planner makes the effort, by thoughtfully considering the entire scope of the plan at hand, to make a realistic assessment of what might happen.

The second is to be able to immediately adapt and adjust to what really does happen. In it's most basic form, this can be called improvisation, which is simply taking actions that weren't planned. Generally, when improvisation occurs where a plan is already in place, it's a good idea to revisit the plan and modify it accordingly, taking into account what is really happening and how that will impact the overall plan going forward.

In this scenario, the planners should also review the thinking that ultimately failed to predict the actual occurrences, in an attempt to minimize any additional surprises and benefit future plans.

The reality is that even when the need for improvisation arises, having a good plan in place will generally allow the individual or the team to react to the circumstances more effectively. This is because, with a solid plan in place, nobody is forced to act without any preparation whatsoever. Instead, the reactions are made based on a common understanding of the situation and the expected result (remember Leaders Intent). So even if real world circumstances mandate a deviation from the steps defined by the plan, the intent of the plan and the vision it seeks to implement remain the same. This consistent framework will generally result in improvisation that is in keeping with the planning theory.

The Planning Process

Since the planning process occurs at many different levels, unless you are the CEO, you will receive guidance from your "Higher Commanders." This is the input that will begin the planning process for you, your teams, or your departments. Ideally, your "Higher" (the person you report to) is also utilizing Maneuver Management and will provide you with the appropriate level of guidance and information to begin your own process in the form of a 5P.

If not, that's okay. You will gather the information and plan correctly so all of those below you will be more effective planners and executors. After your boss sees the effectiveness of your methods, give them a copy of this book and then ask for a promotion.

If you are the CEO or top-level planner, you will need to deliver initial inputs to your planning team, or yourself if you're a small business owner without a team. There are any number of ways to do this to varying effectiveness. The initial inputs are not meant to spell out the plan, they are meant to facilitate the creation of the plan. If there is information the planners need and only you have, it must be included with your initial inputs. If there is specific guidance on tasking's, competitors, and Endstate, you will also need to provide that.

I have found the most effective way to provide initial inputs is to use an abbreviated 5P format. Generally, your perspective and direction in the following paragraphs will provide the information necessary for planners to engage the process:

I.   Situation
- a.   General
- b.   Battlespace
- c.   Competition/Obstacles
- d.   Partners/Leverage

II.   Mission

III.   Execution
- a.   Commanders Intent
- b.   Concept of Operations
- c.   Coordinating Instructions

V.   Management
- b.   Chain of Command
- c.   Reporting

All of the inputs should be starting points that guide the planners to a desired Endstate. As you may have supposed, there are a few key elements in these inputs that require some more specific guidance.

The Mission you issue should be as specific as possible, stating what the goals are clearly and succinctly. Your Leaders Intent should, likewise, be very clear and specific. Ambiguity in your Leaders Intent will increase the propensity for the planners to stray from your desired Endstate. Conversely, a well-defined Leaders Intent will allow your planners to operate within a framework of understanding.

It is important to create a higher-level chain of command. You will designate a lead planner and any significant subordinate positions you feel are critical and want filled with specific individuals. By doing so, you are delegating your authority to those people you name. Make it clear that the lead planner is in charge. You do not need to create the entire structure for plan implementation, just put some one in charge of the planning.

Lastly, tell the planners of any reports that you require. If you would like daily updates, convey that. If you would like more formal reports on their findings and progress on a weekly basis, now is the time to say that. Do this in your inputs instead of on the side or in conversation. This will allow the entire planning team an understanding of what you require.

The product of the WGPP is the 5P, so it makes perfect sense to initiate the planning with a familiar and integrated format. Once the full 5P is issued from the planners, lower level planners in departments and units will engage the WGPP using the higher 5P as their input and the cycle will continue to the lowest levels. There is a level at which the WGPP is no longer necessary. The structure and mission of your organization determine that break point.

Generally speaking, organizational leaders at the executive level will engage the WGPP and individuals from the management level down will work exclusively with the 5P as both their planning process and communication tool. Each level down, the plan will become less broad and more granular. At the point it reaches the lower level employees, the plan will be very tactical in nature.

The WGPP

Lets take a moment to discus the planning team. Maneuver Management does not prescribe a specific constitution for a planning team. Organizations vary greatly in size, mission, and makeup. For the small business owner, the planning team may be him or her alone. It might also include the company's CPA, lawyer, or any other number of people that are—or perhaps should be—relevant to the scope of the plan.

Larger organizations may bring together Subject Matter Experts (SMEs), department heads, and consultants. Just as each subordinate level plan will become less broad, so to will the compilation of skillsets required for the planning team.

For example, when the accounting department convenes a planning session, they may only require accounting staff to successfully engage in the process. Planning undertaken by the CEO on the other hand would require SMEs from many aspects of the business.

The WGPP consists of 6 phases, they are:

1. Mission Analysis
2. Course of Action Development
3. Course of Action What If
4. Course of Action Comparison and Decision
5. Plan Development
6. Plan Implementation

1. Mission Analysis

In business, the mission analysis defines whatever initiative is under consideration that requires formal planning. During mission analysis, the planner reviews and analyzes everything available regarding the situation, and the outcome that the team intends to shape.

At the conclusion of the mission analysis, the planning team creates a mission statement that defines the specific purpose of the plan, as well as a refined statement of Leaders Intent. These documents establish the vision of what is to be accomplished, and a broad framework within which to accomplish it.

An important aspect of both the mission statement and statement of Leaders Intent is that both elements are specifically intended to allow the planners significant flexibility in the development of the plans. Additionally, the personnel responsible for actually executing the plans have broad latitude within which to exercise personal initiative for contingencies not specifically addressed in the plan itself. Because these elements form the foundation going forward, a review with the principal is warranted.

2. Course of Action—Development

A course of action (COA) is simply a broadly stated potential solution to an assigned mission. Typically, for any given mission there will be multiple courses of action that must be evaluated and compared.

In order to formulate these courses of actions, the planners rely on the mission statement and Leaders Intent. The leader also provides planning guidance for the course of action.

Particularly in civilian business, it is important to understand that at this step the proposed course of action is general and conceptual. It is here where the planners brainstorm different approaches in order to isolate the specific one that is most likely to work.

Each proposed course of action is then examined to ensure that it is feasible, acceptable, distinguishable, and complete with respect to the mission at hand, as well as to the Leaders Intent.

3. Course of Action—What If

Once several courses of action have been developed, what-if each one in order to determine feasibility and probability of success. What-if simulation is simply working through the course of action considering the consequences, positive and negative, of each step. It allows the team to gain a common understanding of how elements in the Battlespace may react. What-if simulation provides the basis for the ultimate decision regarding which specific course of action to follow.

In the military, wargaming (what-if simulating) is a disciplined, interactive process that examines the execution of friendly courses of action in relation to the enemy. At its most refined level, wargaming includes a thinking enemy in the form of a "red cell" that essentially assumes the role of the enemy commander responding to the various proposed courses of action.

Although the WGPP simulation is generally much less intensive, I do advocate using a red team/blue team approach to the process if your resources permit, particularly if the planning effort is addressing a competitive problem.

Even if the planning effort is entirely internally facing, the red team/blue team approach is still very effective. In this situation, the blue team presents the company's courses of action that have been sketched out. The red team then functions as "devil's advocates" picking the various approaches apart, and evaluating each from the perspective of likely success. In either scenario, the red team members should not be part of the blue team planning sessions so as to not create bias.

If you are a small business without a staff to do this with you, this is where those trusted advisors and other business owners come in. Use them to be the "Red Cell" for your what-if scenarios and do the same for them. Again, you will both benefit.

4. Course of Action—Comparison and Decision

Once the various courses of action have been defined, the planning team makes recommendations on how to proceed and the decision maker must decide. This step also provides a logical point to reevaluate the mission itself. By reviewing the courses of action that have been developed, deficiencies in terms of clarity of intent or in the understanding of the overall mission will come to light. If the courses of action have been subjected to red team/blue team analysis, both teams typically present their cases and recommendations to the senior manager or executive.

This is an important step because it determines how the plan will ultimately be developed. The rationale is that it is a lot easier to modify a course of action at this point in time than it is to modify the entire plan after it has been written. We must remain flexible, remember, but I can tell you from experience that people tend to get more and more stiff further along the planning process- it's human nature.

5. Plan Development

The Maneuver Management philosophy is that far less resources will be expended to create and evaluate a plan than to simply start implementing any type of organizational initiative. A rigorous planning process is ultimately far more cost effective, in terms of both time and money, than simply acting without it.

It is in this phase that you will populate a 5P with the results of the planning and course of action decisions. Plans should contain only as much detail as required to provide subordinates with the necessary guidance, while allowing them as much freedom of action as possible.

Many business owners—particularly those who own smaller companies—might feel at this point that this planning process is too detailed and complicated for their needs. Many of those individuals prefer to act spontaneously, and cite their success to date as a validation of that approach.

We believe the opposite. The failure—or inability—to plan effectively is a problem that any business intent on growth must address. Many smaller companies hit a plateau in their growth curve after a period of time. More often than not, this plateau identifies a need to move from a freewheeling, loose-entrepreneurial management model to a more structured and professional one. The Maneuver Management planning methodology can help to rectify that problem. There is absolutely no detriment to engaging in the planning process. You will not stifle your entrepreneurial spirit or edge. That's also from personal experience.

An entrepreneurial mentality is key, even in larger organizations. An entrepreneurial management style, however, is often lacking. Individuals operating in an entrepreneurial mindset often have great vision and ideas, but have difficulty getting them out of their head and into the heads of others. This process does just that. The more planning sessions you engage in, the better you will become at communicating vision, ideas, and requirements.

6. Plan Implementation

We know that very often, civilian businesses don't do enough planning. But when they do, far too often an executive team spends an inordinate amount of time developing a detailed plan that never quite makes it out of the executive suite.

This is generally happens for one of two reasons. First, they planned for the sake of planning and the content of the plan has no real world relevance. Second, the plan is too high level or too abstract. It's great for the people who wrote it, but the information it contains is not actionable at lower levels. Maneuver Management solves this.

I really need to stress that the planning process occurs at all levels. It can't be conducted in a vacuum. Once the executive team formulates a plan, they issue it to the next lower level and it is distilled into action items at that level, as well as into a plan to be issued to even lower levels. The process continues "down the line" until the lowest "ranking" member of the organization has an understanding of the mission at hand and their role in accomplishing it. By this point the plan has been translated into the kind of actionable, granular detail that enables someone to actually do something with it.

Far too often, people create plans to go up, not down. A plan is seen as a product to be given to higher ups, not disseminated down through the organization. This is the opposite of what is correct. If you engage in a planning session and create a product to deliver to the CEO, you may demonstrate your understanding of the organization and mission, but you will not aid the organization in executing the plan or accomplishing the mission. The CEO is not going to execute the plan, the employees are. COA recommendations go up, but plans go down the organization.

If you traveled to Iraq or Afghanistan, found a young Marine with nothing on his collar (a private), and asked him what the mission was, he would tell you and he would be right. If you asked the same Marine what his role was, he would again tell you and he would again be right. That private's ability to answer those questions correctly is this very process in action. It is identical in structure though the missions are vastly different.

Every company has its privates too. Whether it's assembly line workers on the shop floor or men and women making deliveries, those are the folks that actually make the company run. (Just as Marine privates are the ones winning the battles.) In both cases, they can't do their jobs alone. It is essential that both Marine commanders and senior business executives and managers understand the role that the privates play, and empower them to do their jobs.

If you ask the man or woman running your mailroom what the company mission is, would they know? Would they know what their role is in accomplishing that mission and how it impacts mission accomplishment? How about a new customer service representative toiling away in a cubicle? Maybe it's the kid stocking the shelves, or the cashier collecting money.

If not, work your way up through the "ranks" and take note of the first level at which you find the right answers. How high you get will tell you whether you need Maneuver Management today or yesterday. Regardless, if your business is growing rapidly I can almost guarantee you you'll need it tomorrow.

The reality is that while effective planning is the first step in creating positive change, it is just that—a step along the way. To really effect change, the company must also be able to execute. Planning and execution go hand in hand. And from the Maneuver Management perspective, the ability to execute is almost entirely dependent on the ability to lead.

Chapter 10

The 3 D's of a Successful Leader

In the early phases of military service, young officers are introduced into the environment through a rigorous training program that encompasses professional skills, mentoring, execution, and leadership. They are thrust into positions of responsibility that often far exceed levels their civilian peers will encounter. They work in complex organizations and environments, typically performing highly specialized functions.

Young officers often find themselves managing relatively large numbers of even more specialized service members. In order to perform this role, they are trained in the use and development of standardized processes. All of these factors contribute to developing attributes that are fitting for military leaders.

Among the attributes developed, we find the "3 D's." It is these three components of an individual's work ethic that will enable them to learn and function within the environments they will be exposed to. The Three D's — Drive, Dedication, and Discipline—are attributes that already exist in an individual and are further developed to help them succeed. The 3 D's are equally important in business and, in fact, in life.

It's no only important for you to look inward and analyze the condition of the 3 D's in yourself, but it's also important to look for them in your employees. Once you identify them, you can develop them.

Drive

Drive can be defined as the desire to excel under any circumstance, to accomplish the mission, and to be the best possible; it is the will to overcome challenges and succeed.

Well-ingrained drive enables individuals to not only aspire to higher thresholds of competency and performance, but to actually achieve them.

Where a person with common aspirations may find a plateau, a driven person finds only a small ledge. This quality pushes individuals to higher levels of learning and achievement through their desire to be better than the competition.

Dedication

Dedication is the singular commitment to an organization, mission, or cause. It can be further defined as a commitment that is beyond influence or failure. Dedication is a quality that enables organizations to function through adversity and challenges. The more dedicated its members, the more likely an organization is to succeed.

It is an unwavering focus on something, an unshakable faith that the desired outcomes will be achieved. A dedicated individual goes the extra mile to ensure that the mission is accomplished or that the organization improves.

A dedicated person goes beyond the call of duty. They gladly spend time and energy, committing wholeheartedly to the success of the organization.

A dedicated individual makes the mission and the people they are responsible for a priority in their life. They put the good of the organization first, and prioritize it above their own personal comfort.

In civilian organizations, employees often see their position as merely a job—something they do to make money in order to survive. They may see their position as a cog in the wheel and essentially unimportant in the grand scheme of things.

A dedicated employee sees things differently. They see their position as a vital and important contribution to the organization. They identify and find value in their work where less dedicated individuals simply do not. They also make personal sacrifices to complete the tasks at hand in order to enhance the organizational performance. In short, a truly dedicated individual puts the organization first.

It is especially important to lead your most dedicated employees. These people will go to the ends of earth for you and do whatever it takes to get the job done, but they will also have the potential to burn out. A dedicated, but burnt out employee is no better than a lazy, unmotivated one. In fact, they can be worse.

Instead of not doing anything, they will continue to attempt to work, but will do so ineffectively—that can set you back. As leaders, we also want to see our people succeed in their personal lives. Lead them well, reward them, help them find balance, and keep them in your organization.

Discipline

Discipline is the commitment of an individual to operate by a set of rules. These rules most often include a compilation of institutional expectations and requirements as well as personally imposed routines, goals, and values. Discipline starts with the individual, however. Even if the organization imposes no rules or restrictions whatsoever, a disciplined person still abides by their own value structure and set of personal principles.

Discipline is what enables an individual to function in complex, demanding, stressful, and chaotic environments. It also allows them to function effectively in environments where there are no external pressures applied.

Many things are affected by the exercise of personal discipline. Not only does it keep organizations on track and functioning, but it is also what contributes to a person realizing their aspirations and fulfilling their personal dreams.

It is human nature to crave accomplishment and personal fulfillment. A person might want to be physically fit, to obtain a Masters Degree, get a promotion, raise a family, retire comfortably—the list is nearly endless. Regardless of the goal and whatever their aspirations may be, discipline is one of the most vital and important keys to achieving these personal goals.

A disciplined person is able to operate in free form, fluid environments because they have the ability to create structure and order. They also have the ability to prioritize and execute in a fashion that will more predictably attain results.

I should also point out that while these traits will be found in virtually every effective leader, they are also personal traits that will enable a company to prosper. The management of a business seeking to create a cohesive and capable team with a well-defined culture must foster and encourage these traits in every employee. Every leader should strive to infuse his or her team with drive, determination, and discipline as a part of the ongoing development of vital human capital.

Chapter 11

The Road Ahead

We find ourselves in tough times, tougher than we've seen in more than half a century. The marketplace is arguably more dynamic now than ever. Globalization impacts the way almost every business operates and even the way entire economies function. It's critical that your organization has the ability to plan and communicate, manage resources, and develop leadership.

Your competition may or may not understand this, but if they do then you are at risk of being made irrelevant, unless you do it better. If they don't, you will take advantage of that.

It's time to take control of your organization. It's time to be a leader and develop leaders in your organization. By using Maneuver Management, you will create effective plans, communicate your plans clearly, lead and manage more effectively, take action on purpose, and ultimately guide your organization to success.

By implementing Maneuver Management, your organization will create the conditions for success. Your entire organization will use the tools and methods of Maneuver Management to cohesively contribute to the success of the organization.

For that to occur, you must be a leader in your organization. It takes someone to initiate change and that person is you. By starting with yourself and mastering the concepts contained herein, you will be ready to bring change to your organization and facilitate success.

Over the next week, use the WGPP and 5P tool by yourself. It doesn't matter what the subject of the plan is, just engage in it. Start small and grow to bigger and bigger planning efforts.

Next week, issue your first 5P plan to your employees, department, or team. Grow into teaching them how to distill and use your 5P to execute.

The week after that, engage your employees, department, or team in the WGPP and full use of the 5P.

At the end of the month, fully implement the tools and make them standard for planning and communication.

As you integrate Maneuver Management into your organization, use the leadership and strategic thinking concepts presented herein to refine your team, identify leaders, and develop everyone.

Implementation will inherently require a change in your personal habits. You will need to allow additional time (a resource) for planning and communication, initially, as your organization learns the system. Once learning is achieved, the time required will be greatly reduced. In fact, you will find efficiency in the process and also created by the results.

Take responsibility for this change and the results. Every change requires a champion and the most beneficial changes create more and more champions as people are exposed to it. As you spread Maneuver Management in your organization, identify the leaders who will assist you with wider implementation and give them the authority, knowledge, and support they will need to get it done.

Ensure you create and track results through metrics. Performance, understanding of the mission, and time are all possible measurements, but you will need to identify what makes sense for your organization. Ensure you are receiving information on implementation and effectiveness of the system.

I know from personal experience that these methods and tools work and I know they will work for you as well. It's to time to engage.

By the way, if you think this is too complicated, look back over this chapter. You just read an abbreviated 5P. I am purposely leaving out the sub-paragraph indents, i.e. "a. General," "b. Battlespace." See if you can identify them.

I.   Situation

      We find ourselves in tough times; tougher than we've seen in more than half a century. The marketplace is arguably more dynamic now than ever. Globalization impacts the way almost every business operates and even the way entire economies function. It's critical that your organization has the ability to plan and communicate, manage resources, and develop leadership.

Your competition may or may not understand this, but if they do then you are at risk of being made irrelevant, unless you do it better. If they don't, you will take advantage of that.

II.   Mission

It's time to take control of your organization. It's time to be a leader and develop leaders in your organization. By using Maneuver Management, you will create effective plans, communicate your plans clearly, lead and manage more effectively, take action on purpose, and ultimately guide your organization to success.

III.   Execution

By implementing Maneuver Management, your organization will create the conditions for success. Your entire organization will use the tools and methods of Maneuver Management to cohesively contribute to the success of the organization.

For that to occur, you must be a leader in your organization. It takes someone to initiate change and that person is you. By starting with yourself and mastering the concepts contained herein, you will be ready to bring change to your organization and facilitate success.

Over the next week, use the WGPP and 5P tool by yourself. It doesn't matter what the subject of the plan is, just engage in it. Start small and grow to bigger and bigger planning efforts.

Next week, issue your first 5P plan to your employees, department, or team. Grow into teaching them how to distill and use your 5P to execute.

The week after that, engage your employees, department, or team in the WGPP and full use of the 5P.

At the end of the month, fully implement the tools and make them standard for planning and communication.

As you integrate Maneuver Management into your organization, use the leadership and strategic thinking concepts presented herein to refine your team, identify leaders, and develop everyone.

IV.   Admin and Logistics

Implementation will inherently require a change in your personal habits. You will need to allow additional time (a resource) for planning and communication, initially, as your organization learns the system. Once learning is achieved, the time required will be greatly reduced. In fact, you will find efficiency in the process and also created by the results.

V.   Management

Take responsibility for this change and the results. Every change requires a champion and the most beneficial changes create more and more champions as people are exposed to it. As you spread Maneuver Management in your organization, identify the leaders who will assist you with wider implementation and give them the authority, knowledge, and support they will need to get it done.

Ensure you create and track results through metrics. Performance, understanding of the mission, and time are all possible measurements, but you will need to identify what makes sense for your organization. Ensure you are receiving information on implementation and effectiveness of the system.

So, there it is folks- Maneuver Management. Get ready, mount up, and go take the hill- success is waiting.

www.ingramcontent.com/pod-product-compliance
Lightning Source LLC
Chambersburg PA
CBHW051328170526
45166CB00002B/721